Developing Intelligences through Literature

Developing Intelligences through Literature

Ten Theme-Based Units for Growing Minds

Laura Rose

Zephyr
Press®

REACHING THEIR HIGHEST POTENTIAL
Tucson, Arizona

Developing Intelligences through Literature
Ten Theme-Based Units for Growing Minds

Grades K–6

© 1996 by Zephyr Press
Printed in the United States of America

ISBN 1-56976-029-2

Editors: Stacey Lynn and Stacey Shropshire
Cover: Nancy Taylor
Design and production: Daniel Miedaner

Zephyr Press
P.O. Box 66006
Tucson, Arizona 85728-6006

Library of Congress Cataloging-in-Publication Data are available.

Contents

Acknowledgments   xii

Section 1: An Explanation   xiii

Introduction   xiv

    It's Time to Teach Thinking—Again   xiv

    Re-Examining What We Mean by Thinking   xiv

    Reaching and Teaching All Students   xv

    A Workable Model   xv

    Correlation with Gardner's Seven Intelligences   xvi

    The Developing Intelligences through Literature Model   xvi

    How to Use This Book   xix

Section 2: The Units   1

Unit 1: Animal Adventures   3

    Overview   3

    Synopsis of *Rosie's Walk*   5

    Explanation of Unit Focus: Animal Adventures   5

    Cross-Curricular Connections   5

    Special Considerations   5

    To Start the Unit   5

    Literature Connections   6

    Lesson 1: Free Reading with Literature Connections   7

    Lesson 2: Favorite Read-Alouds   7

    Lesson 3: Animal Songs   8

    Lesson 4: Pocket Chart   9

    Lesson 5: Student Illustrations   10

    Lesson 6: Acting Out the Words   12

    Lesson 7: Signing a Story   13

    Lesson 8: Plan and Perform   14

    Lesson 9: Class Research Project   15

Lesson 10: Imagine a Runaway Story 17

Lesson 11: Critical Attribute Game 19

Lesson 12: A Barnyard Map 21

Materials 22

Unit 2: Rhyming 29

Overview 29

Synopsis of *A-Hunting We Will Go* 31

Explanation of Unit Focus: Rhyming 31

Cross-Curricular Connections 31

To Start the Unit 31

Literature Connections 32

Lesson 1: Free Reading with Literature Connections 33

Lesson 2: Favorite Read-Alouds 33

Lesson 3: Learn Mother Goose and Other Rhymes 34

Lesson 4: Signing to Poems 35

Lesson 5: Poem of the Week 36

Lesson 6: Personal Poetry Books 37

Lesson 7: Poetry Sequencing 39

Lesson 8: Singing Rhyme Songs 40

Lesson 9: Write a Song 41

Lesson 10: Jump-Rope Rhymes 42

Materials 44

Unit 3: Solving Problems Together 49

Overview 49

Synopsis of *Jaime O'Rourke and the Big Potato* 52

Explanation of Unit Focus: Solving Problems Together 52

Cross-Curricular Connections 52

To Start the Unit 52

Literature Connections 53

Lesson 1: Free Reading with Literature Connections 55

Lesson 2: Favorite Read-Alouds 55

Lesson 3: Solving Problems Together 56

Lesson 4: Lifting Heavy Objects 57

Lesson 5: Transporting Heavy Objects 59

Lesson 6: Problem-Solving Homework 61

Lesson 7: Potatoes, Potatoes 63

Lesson 8: A Musical Problem 64

Lesson 9: Solving a School Problem 65

Lesson 10: Cooperative Problem-Solving Lessons   66

    10A: Cross the River   67

    10B: Find the Pattern   68

    10C: Menu Problems   69

    10D: Candy Store Problems   71

Lesson 11: Sequencing on the Wall   72

Materials   74

Unit 4: Reading Number Words   81

Overview   81

Synopsis of *Over in the Meadow*   83

Explanation of Unit Focus: Reading Number Words   83

Cross-Curricular Connections   83

To Start the Unit   83

Literature Connections   84

Lesson 1: Free Reading with Literature Connections   85

Lesson 2: Favorite Read-Alouds   85

Lesson 3: Adding Music   86

Lesson 4: Which One?   87

Lesson 5: Singing Number Songs   88

Lesson 6: Personal Graphs   89

Lesson 7: Writing Number Books   91

Lesson 8: Calendar Big Book   93

Lesson 9: Write a Number Song   94

Lesson 10: Read the Story on the Wall   97

Materials   99

Unit 5: Courage   105

Overview   105

Synopsis of *The Bears on Hemlock Mountain*   107

Synopsis of *Keep the Lights Burning, Abbie*   107

Explanation of Unit Focus: Courage   107

Cross-Curricular Connections   107

To Start the Unit   107

Literature Connections   108

Lesson 1: Response Journals   110

Lesson 2: Free Reading with Literature Connections   111

Lesson 3: Favorite Read-Alouds   112

Lesson 4: I Am Proud   113

Lesson 5: Sing a Chant   114

Lesson 6: Acts of Courage   115
Lesson 7: Instant Research   116
Lesson 8: Building Lighthouses   117
Lesson 9: Venn Diagrams   119
Lesson 10: Plan and Perform   121
Lesson 11: Courage Is   122
Materials   124

Unit 6: Needs of Children through Time and Space   131
Overview   131
Synopsis of *When I Was Young in the Mountains*   133
Explanation of Unit Focus:
 Needs of Children through Time and Space   133
Cross-Curricular Connections   133
To Start the Unit   133
Literature Connections   134
Lesson 1: Free Reading with Literature Connections   136
Lesson 2: Favorite Read-Alouds   136
Lesson 3: Common Needs   137
Lesson 4: Then and Now   138
Lesson 5: Then and Now Books   140
Lesson 6: Artifacts   141
Lesson 7: Artifacts Homework   143
Lesson 8: Grandparents' Childhood   144
Lesson 9: Artifacts Field Trip   146
Lesson 10: Comparing Music   147
Lesson 11: Toys and Games   148
Materials   150

Unit 7: Milestones in Growing Up   157
Overview   157
Synopsis of *Pig Pig Grows Up*   159
Explanation of Unit Focus: Milestones in Growing Up   159
Cross-Curricular Connections   159
To Start the Unit   159
Literature Connections   160
Lesson 1: Free Reading with Literature Connections   162
Lesson 2: Favorite Read-Alouds   162
Lesson 3: Growing-up Books   163
Lesson 4: Alike and Different   165

Lesson 5: Sequencing   167
Lesson 6: Plan and Perform the Story   168
Lesson 7: Parent Interview   170
Lesson 8: Plus and Minus   172
Lesson 9: Imagine an Ending to a Greek Myth   173
Lesson 10: Venn Diagrams   175
Materials   178

Unit 8: Making Difficult Decisions   187
Overview   187
Synopsis of *Save Queen of Sheba*   189
Explanation of Unit Focus: Making Difficult Decisions   189
Cross-Curricular Connections   189
Response Journals   189
To Start the Unit   189
Literature Connections   190
Lesson 1: Response Journals   191
Lesson 2: Free Reading Choices   193
Lesson 3: Living on a Wagon   194
Lesson 4: What's in a Name?   195
Lesson 5: Why "Westward, Ho!"?   196
Lesson 6: Westward, Ho! Posters   198
Lesson 7: Pioneer Music and Dance   199
Lesson 8: Writing a Camp Song   200
Lesson 9: Decisions and Consequences   201
Lesson 10: Best Decisions   203
Materials   205

Unit 9: Heroic Fantasy Adventures   211
Overview   211
Synopsis of *Abel's Island*   214
Explanation of Unit Focus: Heroic Fantasy Adventures   214
Cross-Curricular Connections   214
Use of the Lessons That Follow   214
Response Journals   214
To Start the Unit   215
Literature Connections   216
Lesson 1: Response Journals   217
Lesson 2: Free Reading Choices   219
Lesson 3: A Real Island Home   220

Lesson 4: Abel's Boat   222

Lesson 5: Mouse House   223

Lesson 6: Critical Attributes of Plants   224

Lesson 7: Edible Plant Research   226

Lesson 8: The Hero's Journey   227

Lesson 9: More Heroes' Journeys   230

Lesson 10: Compare with *Beauty and the Beast*   231

Lesson 11: Writing Your Own Hero's Journey   232

Lesson 12: Personification   234

Lesson 13: Heroic Music   235

Materials   236

Unit 10: Pet Ownership   241

Overview   241

Synopsis of *Where the Red Fern Grows*   243

Explanation of Unit Focus: Pet Ownership   243

Cross-Curricular Connections   243

Response Journals   243

To Start the Unit   243

Literature Connections   244

Lesson 1: Response Journals   245

Lesson 2: Free Reading with Literature Connections   247

Lesson 3: Saving Money   248

Lesson 4: Pet Bulletin Board and Scrapbooks   249

Lesson 5: Pet Research   251

Lesson 6: Guesses and Facts Double Entry   252

Lesson 7: Appalachian Music   254

Lesson 8: Veterinary Visit   255

Lesson 9: Comparing the Book and a Movie   256

Lesson 10: Joys and Burdens   257

Materials   258

Section 3: Techniques   266

Technique 1: Free Reading with Literature Connections   267

Technique 2: Read-Alouds   268

Technique 3: Music Connections   270

Technique 4: Making Pocket Charts   271

Technique 5: Teacher-Made Books   273

Technique 6: Sign Language   276

Technique 7: Intentions and Reflections   277

Technique 8: Book Groups   278

Technique 9: Visualization   280

Technique 10: Response Journals   281

Technique 11: Writing Opinion Papers   282

Technique 12: Thoughtful Book Reports   284

Technique 13: Webbing for Research Reports   286

Section 4: Conclusion   288

Section 5: Create Your Own Units Using This Model   290

Select a Central Work of Literature and a Focus   291

Brainstorm a Related Literature List   292

Decide How to Present the Literature to Your Students   292

Teach and Enjoy   292

Appendixes

A: A Brief Synopsis of Howard Gardner's Seven Intelligences   294

B: Reference Books for Locating Children's Books by Topic   296

Acknowledgments

In 1993 the administration, staff, and school board of Cutten Elementary School District determined that their first priority would be to take up the challenge of California's *It's Elementary* reform document to "make a rich, meaning-centered, thinking curriculum the centerpiece of instruction for all grade levels." At that time I was designing for Zephyr Press a lesson-planning model to help teachers achieve both variety and balance in the kinds of thinking they stimulate in their students.

The Cutten staff and I worked together during the 1993–1994 school year to explore this Developing Intelligences through Literature model. In our planning sessions, we shared the best activities that we had each found to increase our students' understanding and thoughtful interaction with literature. Then in grade-level groups, we selected works of literature on which to focus and develop each unit. Together we created unit plans based on these selected works of literature, field-tested our ideas, evaluated and revised them. The units in this book are the result of our collaboration.

I would like to thank sincerely all teachers in all classrooms of the world who give so freely and generously of their time to seek new and ever better ways to awaken their students to ever higher realms of thought and action. Few people are truly aware of these ongoing efforts, and fewer still offer teachers the thanks that are so well deserved.

My special thanks go to the staff and administration of Cutten Elementary School District, who once more afforded me the great pleasure of working with their deeply dedicated and richly talented group: Jim Hendry, Marianne Rudebock, Kathy Banducci, Mary DeWald, Charlotte Cables, Suzanne Isom, Fran Moriarty, Patricia Correia, Diane Adan, Rhonda Duskin, Barbara Hickox, Karen Rice, Steven Sipma, Michael Franklin, Pamela Malloy, Carol Roach, Linda Forbes, Julie Osborne, Paula Parodi, Jeri Hoopes, Gregory Morse, Marya Naumann, Teresa Baginski, Scott Nelson, and Marilyn Bilderback.

My deep thanks and appreciation go also to Jo Ann Bauer and Neila Gann, two children's librarians of extraordinary dedication and expertise, who generously helped to compile the literature connections lists that accompany each unit.

We are delighted to share the results of our work with you.

Section 1

An Explanation

Education is not the filling of a pail, but the lighting of a fire.

—William Butler Yeats

Introduction

It's Time to Teach Thinking—Again

One of the phrases on the lips of nearly every educational expert is "We ought to be teaching children how to think." In spite of this acknowledged need, most preservice and inservice training teaches teachers how to think; how to plan lessons; how to get children into, through, and beyond literature; how to assess and remediate; but specific strategies that effectively get the children thinking are all too seldom addressed.

Re-Examining What We Mean by Thinking

It is time to reconsider what we mean when we say that we want students to learn to think. New information from both brain research and educational philosophy suggests that thinking is not merely something the brain does in order to solve a certain kind of puzzle or to deduce main ideas or bias. Thinking is a whole-body experience, including muscular and sensory apparatus, and there are many, many different aspects of the human thought process.

The argument over whether we are sufficiently teaching our students how to think often stems from a too-narrow definition of thinking. One faction defines thinking as logic, another as social conscience, some define genuine thinking as creativity and the ability to diverge from the norm, and still others see the most important student thinking as mastery of basic skills. Proponents of logical thinking have their own vocabulary of induction, deduction, extrapolation, analogies, and metacognition. Benjamin Bloom suggested his ascending levels of thinking: knowledge, comprehension, application, analysis, synthesis, and evaluation. Mary Meeker proposed a complex structure of the intellect. Howard Gardner has suggested that there are seven intelligences: linguistic, musical, logical-mathematical, spatial, bodily-kinesthetic, interpersonal, and intrapersonal. All these paradigms help us understand that there is a deep and rich complexity in human thinking.

The question is not whether we teach thinking in our classrooms (we do), but how we can develop and support a variety of important kinds of thinking process through our daily teaching, given the maze of frameworks and ideologies about how to expand thinking skills.

Reaching and Teaching All Students

If we diligently strive to include a wide variety of thinking processes in our language arts lessons, many more kinds of learners will feel at home in the learning process. All students can learn that they are valuable and competent when they are given frequent opportunities to practice learning through their areas of natural strength. All learners will also be challenged daily to use their brains in new and exciting ways, thus increasing their potential for a wider range of thinking capabilities. Considerable evidence exists that the capacity and the actual size of the brain grow when children are given a wide variety of thinking opportunities.

Unfortunately, the complexity and variety of myriad thinking models often serve as barriers to their transfer into daily classroom practice, and the frequent teaching of many types of thinking that does go on in most classrooms is seldom acknowledged or systematically built upon.

The study of children's literature offers us an excellent curricular area to deliberately employ thought-based strategies because good children's books are full of topics that are meaningful to children and ideas that are worthy of deep consideration. The exemplary units provided for you in this teaching manual are built upon a model that is designed to simplify the task of systematically including a rich and meaningful variety of student thinking and personal involvement through teaching literature-based units.

A Workable Model

To provide a simple, manageable framework for this model, I borrowed from the tried-and-true four categories used by Bruce Joyce to classify teaching strategies. I slightly altered Joyce's original terminology to mastery, personal connection, reasoning, and creation to fit my use of them as thinking processes (see figure I-1).

The addition of one more kind of thinking—metacognition—is vital to students' learning how to take conscious charge of their own thinking processes. *Metacognition* means thinking about our own thinking, deciding what kind of thinking is needed in a given situation, evaluating whether our thinking strategies are effective or

Figure I-1. Bruce Joyce's categories of teaching strategies

whether they should be expanded. Because metacognition can be used to enhance awareness and personal ownership of any other kind of thinking strategy, I placed it in the center of the model (see figure I-2).

Once this framework is laid, nearly every kind of thinking skill or activity can be classified predominantly within one of these five domains (see figure I-3).

Figure I-2. Metacognition added to Joyce's model

Correlation with Gardner's Seven Intelligences

One of the more captivating of current frameworks that address the importance of teaching to a variety of thinking and learning styles is Howard Gardner's theory of multiple intelligences. Gardner suggests that there are many kinds of intelligence; he has identified seven. See appendix A for a brief explanation of each intelligence. The bibliography also offers books for further study.

Because many teachers are searching for teaching materials to help them include these seven intelligences, every unit includes lessons that utilize all seven intelligences. It is easy to include Gardner's intelligences because, like Joyce's four domains, they do not invent excellent teaching; they merely make us aware of the basic elements of good teaching and make it possible for us to engage in it more frequently. Figure I-4 illustrates the correlation between the two theories.

The Developing Intelligences through Literature Model

The ten literature-based, cross-curricular units in this book are designed to engage the greatest number of students by deliberately including all kinds of student thinking styles and a wide variety of output modalities. Each unit spans several grade levels to work well in multiage and multiability classrooms.

The lessons were designed so that each addresses a variety of modalities. There are more lessons in each unit than would usually be practical to employ, so they are clearly keyed to the five thinking domains and the seven intelligences. You can select a range from among the lessons offered so students will experience a variety of thinking processes within each unit.

Figure I-3. The thinking skills that fit into Joyce's model

Creating a Meaningful Focus

Good literature is full of ideas that are worth thinking about. It is meant to move the mind and stir the emotions, to broaden the range of human experience and human compassion. The central literature selection for a unit of study is essentially a device to help all students focus on important ideas that are intrinsically interesting and meaningful. The units in this book are not built merely upon a particular book, but on its focus or central idea. Students read independently many other books related to the unit.

One of the basic tenets of the whole language approach is that children will learn to read by reading a rich variety of books of their own selection and at their own level of individual ability. Yet as important and copious individual "free" reading is to the development of active and enthused readers, there is still a vital place for teacher-directed units based on a work of literature that the whole class reads.

Figure I-4. Correlation with the Seven Intelligences theory

Because students in any classroom are likely to be at different reading levels, each student does not need to read the central book. When you read the book aloud, the entire class will have a common, positive literature experience around which to share ideas, to express opinions, to explore possibilities, to disagree, to come together.

Making Cross-Curricular Connections

I have attempted to include other curricular areas in each unit wherever they naturally fit. Each unit preview offers suggestions about how it might blend with other curricular objectives. Each lesson identifies any such connections.

Perfect for the Multiage Classroom

Even classes that are not labeled as such are in fact multiage and multiability. When you read aloud the central literature selection, students of all ages and abilities can join in the discussion and open-ended activities regardless of personal reading ability.

Using with Special Students

Because the units span several grade levels, you may use the suggestions given for use with earlier grades to modify assignments for special needs students and those for later grades to challenge the gifted.

How to Use This Book

The next section of this book contains ten fully developed, thoughtful, meaning-centered unit plans that you can use in either single-grade or multiage classrooms. Although the lessons are arranged in an approximate order, you may select and rearrange them to suit your students' needs and your teaching style.

You need not do all of the lessons in a unit. A variety is offered so that you can select those that best fit your students' needs and your own teaching style and circumstances.

Each unit contains the following:

- A central literature selection and a synopsis of its story
- The thoughtful focus selected for the unit
- A range of grade levels for which the unit is appropriate
- A list of books (literature connections) on the topic of the unit's focus for your students to read
- Detailed lesson plans labeled with appropriate grade levels and thinking-skills connections
- The approximate time each lesson will take
- Work sheets needed for all lesson plans
- Ideas for making cross-curricular connections
- Adaptations of some lessons for use with students of various ages and abilities

In section 3 you will find a detailed description of a number of specific techniques that are used in some of the unit lesson plans. Each technique stands on its own as an effective teaching strategy. They are in their own section so you can refer to them easily and apply them in learning situations other than the units. These techniques were included because of their strength in evoking or supporting the use of thinking skills from each of the four domains and because of their deliberate inclusion of the seven intelligences.

Section 2

The Units

Reading is a basic tool in the living of a good life.

—Mortimer J. Adler

Unit 1

OVERVIEW

Central Literature Selection:

Rosie's Walk

by Pat Hutchins

Unit Focus: Animal Adventures

Grades: K–2

THINKING SKILLS SYMBOLS IDENTIFICATION				
Personal Connection	Creation	Mastery	Reasoning	Metacognition

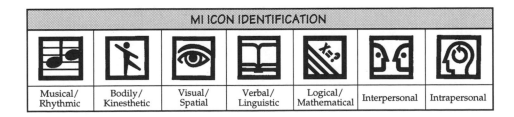

MI ICON IDENTIFICATION						
Musical/ Rhythmic	Bodily/ Kinesthetic	Visual/ Spatial	Verbal/ Linguistic	Logical/ Mathematical	Interpersonal	Intrapersonal

Lesson 1:   **Free Reading with Literature Connections** (Grades 1–2; a few minutes a day)
Students spend time each day reading, discussing unit-centered books of their choosing, and telling the class what they enjoyed and why.

Lesson 2:   **Favorite Read-Alouds** (Grades K–2; five to ten minutes a day)
Students keep track of all read-alouds that match the unit and let students vote on their favorites.

Lesson 3:   **Animal Songs** (Grades K–2; five minutes; repeated during unit)
Students learn to sing and read assorted animal songs.

Lesson 4:   **Pocket Chart** (Grades K–2; one class period)
Students practice reading a pocket chart that has words and pictures from the story.

Lesson 5:   **Student Illustrations** (Grades K–2; four or more class periods)
Because there are so few words in the book, students can write and illustrate their own copies.

Lesson 6:   **Acting Out the Words** (Grades 1–2; one or two P.E. class periods)
Students use the directional words such as *over* and *through* to direct actions at P.E. stations.

Lesson 7:   **Signing a Story** (Grades K–2; ten minutes; repeated during the unit)
Students learn to sign the story of *Rosie's Walk*.

Lesson 8:   **Plan and Perform** (Grades K–2; four or more class periods)
Students form groups and present the story of *Rosie's Walk* to the class in a variety of ways, such as shadow puppets, audiotape, or pantomime.

Lesson 9:   **Class Research Project** (Grades 1–2; four or more class periods)
Using simple, effective research strategies, students learn how to pose and answer research questions in their personalized research books.

Lesson 10:   **Imagine a Runaway Story** (Grades K–2; one class period)
Following another animal adventure story, *The Runaway Bunny*, students use their imaginations to write an additional page of the story to put in a class book.

Lesson 11:   **Critical Attribute Game** (Grades K–2; fifteen to twenty minutes)
Students play a reasoning game to guess the teacher's animal classification system.

Lesson 12:   **A Barnyard Map** (Grades 1–2; one class period)
Students draw the action in *Rosie's Walk* as a map.

Synopsis of Rosie's Walk

This picture book has very few words, which makes it a good introduction to reading. The illustrations show Rosie the hen going for a walk, oblivious to the fox who walks behind her and gets into one bit of trouble after another. At the book's end, Rosie returns home in time for dinner, apparently unaware of the unfortunate fox's unsuccessful pursuit. Children find the troubles of the fox hilarious and the story delightful.

Rosie's Walk is so easy to read that most first-graders and even some kindergartners will soon be reading it on their own. From this central selection, students will be engaged in other activities that challenge them to read and write at their own appropriate levels.

Explanation of Unit Focus: Animal Adventures

Each of the books selected for this unit tells of an exciting animal adventure, with which most children readily identify and enjoy.

Cross-Curricular Connections

This unit correlates with any study of farm or wild animals. Several of the lessons lead into this connection. The unit also works well with a study of birds or of egg development and hatching. If you do hatch eggs, students can write a description of the process of hatching and development to read to their parents.

Special Considerations

Kindergarten

You may be able to use many of the lessons more effectively if you are working with a small group instead of with the whole class.

To Start the Unit

Look at the suggested lessons and select those that are appropriate for your class. Read *Rosie's Walk* aloud to your students, then proceed with any lesson you choose.

Literature Connections

Following is a list of books on the unit's focus for your students to read independently during the unit and even after you have finished the unit. If each student is reading a different book, discussions and activities regarding the unit's focus will be far richer than if everyone reads the same selection. See technique 1, Free Reading with Literature Connections, for suggestions.

Books

Carle, Eric. 1972. *The Rooster Who Set Off to See the World*. Franklin Watts.

Conover, Chris. 1989. *Mother Goose and the Sly Fox*. Farrar, Straus, and Giroux.

Ernst, Lisa C. 1992. *Zinnia and Dot*. Viking Child Books.

Galdone, Paul. 1968. *Henny Penny*. Seabury Press. (Any version will do.)

———. 1973. *The Three Billy Goats Gruff*. Ticknor and Fields. (Any version will do.)

Ginsburg, Mirra. 1982. *Across the Stream*. Greenwillow Books.

Heller, Ruth. 1981. *Chickens Aren't the Only Ones*. Grosset and Dunlap.

Jeschke, Susan. 1980. *Perfect the Pig*. Scholastic.

Kanza Keiko. 1987. *Wolf's Chicken Stew*. Putnam.

Kellog, Steven. 1985. *Chicken Little*. William Morrow. (Any version will do.)

Kimmel, Eric A. 1988. *Anansi and the Moss-Covered Rock*. Holiday House.

Leverich, Kathleen. 1978. *The Hungry Fox and the Foxy Duck*. Goodmaster Books.

Lionni, Leo. 1969. *Alexander and the Wind-up Mouse*. Pantheon.

Marshall, James. 1986. *Wings*. Viking.

———. 1989. *The Three Little Pigs*. Dial Books for Young Readers. (Any version will do.)

McClosky, Robert. 1969. *Make Way for Ducklings*. Viking.

McLeish, Kenneth. 1974. *Chicken Licken*. Putnam.

Morris, William Barret. 1970. *The Longest Journey in the World*. Holt.

Pinkwater, Honest Dan'l. 1982. *Roger's Umbrella*. Dutton.

Plume, Ilse. 1980. *The Bremen-Town Musicians*. Doubleday.

Rey, H. A. 1958. *Curious George*. Houghton Mifflin. (The entire series is appropriate.)

Steig, William. 1969. *Sylvester and the Magic Pebble*. Prentice.

———. 1976. *The Amazing Bone*. Farrar, Straus, and Giroux.

Tafuri, Nancy. 1984. *Have You Seen My Ducklings?* Greenwillow Book.

Wells, Rosemary. 1990. *Little Lame Prince*. Dial.

Wildsmith, Brian. 1981. *Bear's Adventure*. Pantheon.

Zion, Gene, 1956. *Harry the Dirty Dog*. Harper.

Lesson 1

FREE READING WITH LITERATURE CONNECTIONS

Materials

books from the literature connections list or any other books that involve animal adventures

Preparation

Gather books on the unit's focus of animal adventures (see Literature Connections, page 6, for suggestions).

Procedure

Every day let students spend ten to fifteen minutes reading and looking at these books. Include any animal adventure books that you have read aloud, as these will be some of the most popular. (See technique 1, Free Reading with Literature Connections, on page 267.)

Multiple Intelligence Connections

Lesson 2

FAVORITE READ-ALOUDS

Materials

read-aloud books from literature connections or other books about animal adventures

Preparation

Photocopy the cover or title page, whichever has a more interesting picture, of each day's read-aloud selection.

Procedure

Each day, read at least one story aloud from your unit-oriented literature collection. See technique 2, Read-Alouds, page 268.

Multiple Intelligence Connections

Lesson 3

ANIMAL SONGS

Materials

chart paper

markers

songs about animal adventures, such as "Six Little Ducks," "Five Green and Speckled Frogs," and "The Fox Went Out on the Town One Night"

optional: 12-by-18-inch white art paper

optional: crayons or felt-tip markers

Preparation

Gather songs and record them in large print on chart paper (see technique 3, Music Connections, page 270).

Procedure

Step 1: Point to words on a song chart as you teach the song to students.

Step 2: Once students know the song, let volunteers point to the words each time the class sings.

Optional Step 2: As a puzzle, cover some words on the chart with self-stick notes and ask students to deduce and write down the words that are covered. This technique teaches students to track.

More Challenge

Step 1: Give each student a copy of one song and a 12-by-18-inch sheet of white art paper. Have them fold the paper in half widthwise and paste the song on one side.

Step 2: While students sing the song again, ask them to get a vivid mental image. Invite them to share some of their images, then ask them to draw their images on the paper facing the song.

Step 3: When students have completed their pictures, sing the song again while students track the words on their papers. Kindergartners may sing without tracking or reading.

Multiple Intelligence Connection

POCKET CHART

Materials

a pocket chart

sentence strips with basic lines from *Rosie's Walk*

cards with changeable words and pictures (see preparation)

Preparation

See technique 4, Making Pocket Charts, on page 271 for directions on making the pocket chart. Make two sentence strips with the first and last lines of *Rosie's Walk*. Also make cards with all of the directional words (*over, around,* and so on), cards with words for each story element (the yard, the pond, and so on), and cards with pictures of each story element (the yard, the pond, and so on).

Procedure

Step 1: To introduce the story, read *Rosie's Walk* from the pocket chart, then put in the first line of the story and read it aloud with students.

Step 2: Hand out all of the word cards and picture cards, giving one to each student volunteer.

Step 3: Read through the book, pause at each page to ask who has the words and picture that match, and let those students come up and put the words and pictures in the pocket chart (see example below).

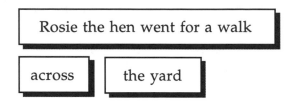

Rosie the hen went for a walk

across | the yard

Step 4: Read the line in the book and on the chart so that the class can check to see if the words are correct. If not, hand them back and try again.

Step 5: Continue until the story is finished (you have read the last line strip).

Step 6: Read the story all the way through on the chart and ask students to imagine the story in their minds' eyes as they read with you.

Leave the pocket chart up for students to work with in free time.

Multiple Intelligence Connections

Lesson 5

STUDENT ILLUSTRATIONS

Materials

teacher-made books with 8 half-sheets of white paper

crayons or felt-tip pens

pencils

optional: a chicken stamp and a fox stamp

Preparation

Make a book for each student (and a few extra copies to cover emergencies). See technique 5, Teacher-Made Books, page 273.

Procedure

Step 1: After reading or reviewing *Rosie's Walk,* give each student a book. Ask students to write the first line of *Rosie's Walk* and illustrate it on their first pages. If you have a chicken stamp, students may stamp chickens on their papers and then draw the background.

Step 2: Have students draw Rosie walking on the left page and the fox getting into trouble on the right page on each following set of facing pages. Students can fit the words in wherever they match. If you have done lesson 3, students can refer to the pocket chart to figure out what goes on each page.

Step 3: After each page is complete with drawing and words, have students raise their hands and read the page to you so any errors can be corrected immediately. (If a spread is very messy and the student is unhappy with it, run a bead of glue around the pages' edges to glue them together; the messy spread will disappear.)

Step 4: When all the directional pages are completed, have students add the line from the last page of *Rosie's Walk* to the last pages of their books.

Step 5: When the books are finished, ask students to work in pairs and read their books to each other. After reading, they should sign the backs of their partners' books. Send the books home to be read to parents and added to home libraries. You might like to include parent note 1-1.

Additional Steps for Kindergarten

- Write the story lines on the first and last pages.
- Students can be given the option to copy the direction words from the teacher's model on the other pages or to ask the teacher to do all of the writing in each book. If you have a large class of kindergartners, you might prefer to write on all the pages yourself and then duplicate and assemble a book for each child.

More Challenge

Let students who wish to do so imagine events other than those in the original story. Ask those students to close their eyes and imagine something else that could be in a farmyard, how Rosie could pass it, and what could happen to the fox. Then those students can draw their creative pictures instead of pictures from the story.

Multiple Intelligence Connections

Lesson 6

ACTING OUT THE WORDS

Materials

assorted P.E. materials

cards using the directional words from *Rosie's Walk*

Preparation

Make a card for each direction word from *Rosie's Walk*. Gather P.E. materials that will match the direction cards (see example below).

Procedure

Step 1: Using materials that will work with the direction cards, set up P.E. stations in a gym or on the playground using the following words.

> *across* goes by balance beam
> *around* goes by a set of traffic cones
> *over* goes by a series of ropes that students can jump over
> *past* goes by sandbox
> *through* goes by a tunnel
> *under* goes by a rope two students hold at waist height

Step 2: Ask for student volunteers to hold the cards. Send the volunteers to appropriate stations.

Step 3: Send the other students through the course. After each student completes one station, she or he goes immediately to the next station. At each station, students must read the word and follow the direction.

Step 4: Change the arrangement of the words and have students repeat the activity.

More Challenge

The next day, add more directional words. Let students decide which words should go with which stations (see figure 1-1). Five or six students could plan an obstacle course, draw it on a map for you to check, and then set up the course and run it the following day.

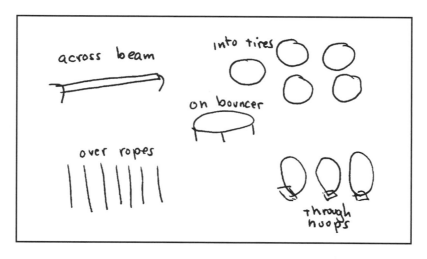

Figure 1-1. An obstacle course to challenge students

Multiple Intelligence Connections

Lesson 7

SIGNING A STORY

Materials for the Teacher

a book of sign language with words from *Rosie's Walk*

Preparation

Do this lesson after reading *Rosie's Walk* several times. Learn the signs for each line of *Rosie's Walk*. Read technique 6, Sign Language, page 276, for suggestions of resources and activities.

Procedure

Step 1: Reread *Rosie's Walk,* teaching the signs for each page as you read.

Step 2: Reread the book as students sign.

Step 3: Continue to read the book from time to time as students sign.

More Challenge

Use this technique with other songs and poems throughout the year.

Multiple Intelligence Connections

Lesson 8

PLAN AND PERFORM

Materials

props students choose to help them act out story

one copy per student of work sheet 1-1, Intentions and Reflections, page 24

Preparation

For grades 1 and 2, photocopy work sheet 1-1. Read technique 7, Intentions and Reflections, on page 277. Read or reread *Rosie's Walk* aloud to your class.

Procedure

Step 1: Ask students to brainstorm ways to act out *Rosie's Walk*. Suggest to them ideas from technique 8, Book Groups, page 278, or other activities you have enjoyed. Model and encourage the addition of musical instruments for sound effects or background music.

Step 2: Divide the class into groups according to performance format preferences. Give them time, materials, and assistance over several class periods to help them prepare their performances.

Step 3 for grades 1 and 2: Have students keep track of their plans and progress on work sheet 1-1. After their performances, students may turn their work sheets over and write at least one thing about their performances of which they are proud.

Step 4: Have each group perform its version of this story while the rest of the class watches. After each performance, ask for volunteers from the class to give at least one compliment.

Optional Step 5: Invite parents to see the performances.

Suggestions for Use with Kindergarten

Do this lesson during station time so each group has adult assistance.

More Challenge

Instead of everyone working on the same story, let groups choose their favorite read-aloud book and select a performance format.

Multiple Intelligence Connections

Lesson 9

CLASS RESEARCH PROJECT

Materials for the Teacher

fact sheet 1-1 on page 25

Materials for Students

teacher-made books with six sheets of lined paper

pencils

Preparation

Make a book of six sheets of lined paper for each student (see technique 5, Teacher-Made Books, page 273).

Procedure

Step 1: Tell students that they are going to research how chickens are born, how they live, what they eat, and other important facts.

Step 2: Ask students to help make a list of questions about chickens for which they wish to learn answers. List these on a chart or bulletin board. Some questions might be

> *How long does it take for an egg to hatch?*
>
> *What do chickens like to eat?*
>
> *Why do chickens eat rocks?*
>
> *How many eggs does a chicken lay?*
>
> *What is the difference between a hen and a rooster?*
>
> *Do baby chickens have feathers?*
>
> *How many different kinds of chickens are there?*
>
> *How big is the littlest chicken and the biggest chicken?*

Step 3: Together, read over the list that the class has made and have students vote on their favorite questions. Limit the list to five or six questions that the whole class will write about.

Step 4: Help students copy the questions into their books, one question per page. This part of the activity may take more than one day.

Step 5: Tell students that you are going to read to them a selection about chickens. Ask students to raise their hands every time they hear you read an answer to one of the questions. You will then stop so that they can write the answer on the appropriate page. You will probably not read the entire fact sheet 1-1 on chickens in one day; you will read until students hear an answer, then you will stop to help students frame and write the answer. Continue reading over the course of two or even three days.

When students stop you, you might want to have them help you phrase the answer and write it correctly on the board so that they can copy it. I don't insist students write entire sentences unless sentences are necessary. If the question is "What do chickens eat?" I allow *grain* and *small insects* for the answers. Otherwise, children get tired of writing and lose enthusiasm for this project.

Students may notice answers to other questions that were not selected for the books. Stop and discuss these as well.

Step 6: When their books are complete, let students read them to each other. If some questions were not answered, consult your librarian, local zoo, or university. Let students know that some research questions cannot be answered; perhaps they will grow up to be scientists and discover the answers.

More Challenge

Ask some or all students to select one or two questions that were not chosen by the class. Invite those students to write their questions on the last few pages of their books and to listen for those answers as well.

Multiple Intelligence Connections

Lesson 10

IMAGINE A RUNAWAY STORY

Materials

work sheet 1-2, Imagine a Runaway Story

The Runaway Bunny by Margaret Wise Brown (referenced in literature connections)

Preparation

Photocopy work sheet 1-2 for each student.

Procedure

Step 1: Read *The Runaway Bunny* aloud to your class.

Step 2: Ask students to close their eyes and pretend that they are the runaway bunny and are looking for a hiding place where the mother bunny will never be able to find them. Give them about thirty seconds to imagine such a place.

Step 3: Ask students to tell you where they went. After many students share their ideas, ask those who did not think of a place to pick one of the places they heard someone else share.

Step 4: Ask students to close their eyes again and pretend that they are the runaway bunny hiding in the place that they have chosen. Remind students that if they haven't thought of a place of their own, they may borrow someone else's idea.

Step 5: Ask them to imagine the mother bunny. Ask them to watch and see how she finds the runaway bunny. What does she have to do? What does she have to become? Give students about thirty seconds of silence to think of their answers.

Step 6: Again ask some students to share what they saw. Then ask for a show of hands of students who could not figure out how the mother could find the runaway bunny; let classmates help those students with ideas. This step ensures that all students have something to write about. (I find that when given options from other students, the child who asked for help will usually create his or her own solution).

Step 7: Give students copies of work sheet 1-2, go over the words with them, and tell them to draw the bunny hiding in the first picture and the mother finding him in the second. Then, ask them to write their ideas in the blanks to tell what is happening.

Step 8: When students finish, collect the pictures, read them aloud to the class, and bind them into a class book to add to your classroom library. Students will love reading their book.

Additional Step for Kindergarten

- Let students dictate their ideas as the teacher records.

Additional Step for First Grade

- Let students dictate their ideas for you to print on paper strips to be copied in their books.

Additional Step for Second Grade

- Students write in their own words and ask for help spelling words they don't know (see example below).

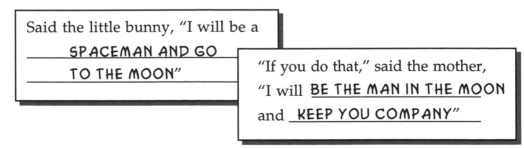

Said the little bunny, "I will be a
SPACEMAN AND GO
TO THE MOON"

"If you do that," said the mother,
"I will BE THE MAN IN THE MOON
and KEEP YOU COMPANY"

Note: This exercise is taken from *Picture This: Teaching Reading through Visualization* by Laura Rose. For more information on the importance of helping students visualize, see technique 9, Visualization, on page 280.

Multiple Intelligence Connections

CRITICAL ATTRIBUTE GAME

Materials for the Teacher

one green and one red 12-by-18-inch piece of construction paper

cards with animal pictures, plastic animals, or any other wide assortment of animals that you may have

Materials for Each Student

one green marker

one red marker

or

one green Unifix cube

one red Unifix cube

Preparation

Get a red and a green marker or Unifix cube for each child. Have ready a sheet of green and a sheet of red construction paper. Gather any sets of animal cards or plastic animals you may have, the greater variety the better.

Before the lesson begins, decide upon a classification system that you wish to use for this lesson, such as animals that have feathers or do not have feathers, animals that lay eggs or give birth, animals that have four legs or that do not have four legs, animals who eat meat or those who do not.

Procedure

Step 1: Give each child a red and a green marker and display the two sheets of construction paper where everyone can see them.

Step 2: Place one animal on the green sheet and another on the red, according to your prearranged classification system. For example, if you decided on wild animals/tame animals, you would place two animals as those in the example below.

Red

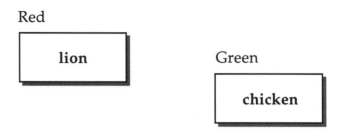

Green

Step 3: Show students another animal, for instance, a deer, and ask them to hold up the color marker that matches the sheet where they think the animal belongs. Ask a few students to tell their reasons so that they can learn thinking strategies from each other. Do not tell them whether their guesses are correct.

Step 4: Without comment, place the next animal on the sheet where it belongs. Then show another animal. Ask students to hold up the color marker that tells where they think this new animal belongs. Again, ask a few students to share their reasons. You can clarify their thinking by saying, "Oh, so you have a color theory," or "It sounds like you have a mammal/not mammal theory," or "You have a theory about farm animals and zoo animals," but do not tell students whether they are right or wrong. Then place this new animal on the correct color for your classification system.

Step 5: Continue this process until most students are guessing correctly each time. Let them tell you what they think your system is, and tell them if they are correct. Learning how to make theories and test them is a valuable part of this lesson and can be repeated with a different classification system every day of your unit.

Multiple Intelligence Connections

Lesson 12

A BARNYARD MAP

Materials

a sheet of chart paper or an overhead transparency

9-by-12-inch sheets of white art paper

crayons or felt-tip pens

Preparation

Read or reread *Rosie's Walk* aloud to your students.

Procedure

Step 1: Tell students that this paper will represent Rosie's barnyard as if they were floating in the sky above it. Read the first page of *Rosie's Walk,* and ask students to help you decide where Rosie's hen house should go. Draw the house on your chart or on the overhead transparency, and have students draw it on their paper.

Step 2: Read the next page of *Rosie's Walk* and ask students where to put the yard and the rake. Decide together and all draw the items on the same parts of the papers. Show students how to draw a red line that traces Rosie's walk thus far.

Step 3: Read the next page and decide together where the pond should go. Remind students that Rosie ends up back where she started, so the path she takes probably needs to be circular. Continue the red line that depicts Rosie's path. Continue this process with each page until Rosie is back where she started.

More Challenge

Students create their own labeled maps of one or more of the other books you have read aloud.

Unit 1

MATERIALS

Dear Parent,

As part of our study of children's literature, your child has written and illustrated this book. He or she should be able to read it to you, and I hope you will take the time to listen to it and discuss the words and the pictures. After your child reads this book to you, perhaps you can add it to your home library of children's books. In the future, you might sometimes choose to read this book along with those by more famous authors.

I hope you enjoy and express your pride in your child's work.

Sincerely,

Work Sheet 1-1
Intentions and Reflections
Adding Metacognition to Projects

Date:_____ Today I intend to _____

_____

_____

_____

During this work period, I was able to _____

_____

_____

Tomorrow I hope to

_____

_____

Date:_____ Today I intend to _____

_____

_____

_____

During this work period, I was able to _____

_____

_____

Tomorrow I hope to

_____

_____

Note: For longer projects, use additional sheets or have students use a teacher-made journal to make similar daily entries.

Developing Intelligences through Literature © 1996 Zephyr Press, Tucson, AZ

Chickens

People have been raising chickens for protein and for eggs for as long as anyone can remember. Chickens were raised in ancient China, Egypt, and Rome, and we are still raising them today. Chickens can survive perfectly well in the wild, but most chickens are now raised on farms or chicken ranches. Chickens will eat almost anything, and many farmers use their chickens as a garbage disposal to eat up all of the table scraps, fruit, and vegetable skins. Chickens are especially fond of grain such as corn and oats, and they must also eat small pebbles from time to time. The pebbles are stored in the gizzard and help to break down the chicken's food by grinding it.

The male chicken is called a *rooster* or *cock,* the female is called a *hen,* and the babies are called *chicks.* The rooster is the one who crows the familiar cock-a-doodle-doo song, and the hen makes many different sounds, from clucking and cackling to squawking. The roosters of all species have sharp spurs that they use in fights with other roosters.

There are hundreds of varieties of chickens of varying sizes and colors. In some species the roosters have long tails, and in others the roosters are short-tailed. The Brahma rooster weighs up to twelve pounds, but the Bantam rooster weighs only a little over one pound.

Chickens are not born alive from their mothers. Like other birds, the mothers lay eggs and sit on them to keep them warm until they hatch. Eggs come in many colors: brown, green, white, and speckled, depending on the type of chicken. The hen has to turn the eggs over three times every day. She only leaves her nest once a day to eat and drink.

A baby chick is ready to hatch in about twenty-one days and it starts peeping the day before it is born. It has a special egg-tooth that helps it peck a hole in the hard eggshell. Getting out is hard work and takes many hours. When the baby chick finally breaks all the way out of the egg, it is tired and wet. Although born with no feathers, it has a warm coat of down. Soon its coat will become fluffy, and the chick will begin exploring. It has sharp eyes right from the first. It can eat and drink on its own, but because it has been so well fed inside the egg, it can go without eating for a whole week.

The hen is a good mother. She sits on her eggs to keep them warm, because if the eggs cool off, the chicks will die. She even pulls out her own chest feathers to make her skin warmer where it rests on the eggs. Once the chicks are hatched, she hovers around them, listening for their little peeps. If one peep is missing, she goes right off to rescue the little chick and bring it back to her brood. She continues to gather them under her wings to keep them warm for several weeks, until they can stand the cooler air on their own.

Developing Intelligences through Literature © 1996 Zephyr Press, Tucson, AZ

A good laying hen can lay more than 275 eggs a year. If she is allowed to hatch her own chicks, she will not lay that many. She will lay around 12 eggs and then stop laying and sit on them until all the chicks are hatched and on their own. When people raise chickens, they often take the eggs from the hens and put the eggs in an incubator to hatch so that the mother hen will keep laying eggs for the farmers to eat or sell. In the incubator the eggs are kept warm and turned until they hatch.

Many animals, such as foxes, weasels, raccoons, and birds of prey, love to eat chickens and their eggs, so a good henhouse and fence must protect the chickens and keep predators out. Chickens do not make good pets, but they have lived with people and given us good food for thousands of years.

Developing Intelligences through Literature © 1996 Zephyr Press, Tucson, AZ

"If you do that," said the mother

"I will _____

and _____ "

Said the little bunny, "I will be a _____

_____ "

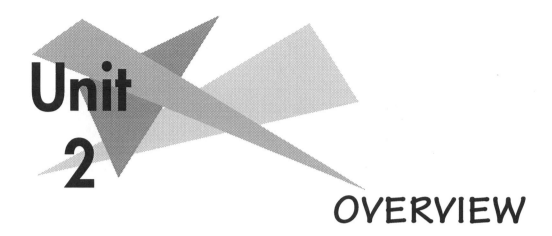

Unit 2

OVERVIEW

Central Literature Selection:

A Hunting We Will Go
by John Langstaff

Unit Focus: Rhyming
Grades: K–2

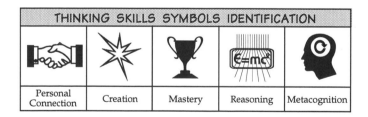

THINKING SKILLS SYMBOLS IDENTIFICATION				
Personal Connection	Creation	Mastery	Reasoning	Metacognition

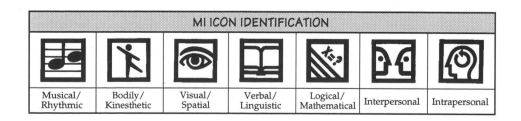

MI ICON IDENTIFICATION						
Musical/ Rhythmic	Bodily/ Kinesthetic	Visual/ Spatial	Verbal/ Linguistic	Logical/ Mathematical	Interpersonal	Intrapersonal

Lesson 1: **Free Reading with Literature Connections** (Grades K–2; twenty minutes a day)

Students spend time each day reading and sharing books related to the unit focus.

Lesson 2: **Favorite Read-Alouds** (Grades K–2; five to ten minutes a day)

Students keep track of all rhyming read-alouds and vote on favorites.

Lesson 3: **Learn Mother Goose and Other Rhymes** (Grades K–2; ten minutes a day)

Students are regularly exposed to traditional and other wonderful children's rhymes through read-aloud selections and free-reading choices.

Lesson 4: **Signing to Poems** (Grades K–2; five minutes; repeated during the unit)

Students learn sign language to accompany some poems.

Lesson 5: **Poem of the Week** (Grades 1–2; ten minutes a day)

This is a year-long plan for memorizing and reciting poetry with parental help.

Lesson 6: **Personal Poetry Books** (Grades 1–2; ten to twenty minutes a week)

In conjunction with the poem of the week program, students post and illustrate their own copies of the poems they are learning. They add a new poem each week and read it to partners on a regular basis.

Lesson 7: **Poetry Sequencing** (Grades 1–2; fifteen minutes a week)

After the poem of the week has been taken down from the board, it can serve as a regular opportunity for student partners to sequence the lines and read them to each other and to the teacher.

Lesson 8: **Singing Rhyme Songs** (Grades K–2; five to ten minutes a day)

Rhyming songs are constructed to invite students to guess the rhyming word. Singing these songs regularly will add to students' rhyming abilities.

Lesson 9: **Write a Song** (Grades 1–2; one to three class periods)

Students help write a song by using a framework such as *A-Hunting We Will Go* and brainstorming new rhyming words for further verses. In their teacher-made books, students write and illustrate the new verses to the song.

Lesson 10: **Jump-Rope Rhymes** (Grades K–2; ten minutes a day)

Students learn and improve upon traditional jump-rope rhymes while jumping rope in P.E. or at recess.

Synopsis of A-Hunting We Will Go

In this picture book version of the old nursery rhyme and song with which most of us are familiar, there is no plot, but just the repeated verse with a different animal and rhyme on each page, for example, "We'll catch a fox and put him in a box," or "We'll catch a goat and put him in a boat." The charm and motivation of this book is in the children's ability to join in with even the first reading.

Explanation of Unit Focus: Rhyming

Because the natural way to learn rhyming is through poetry and song, this book serves as a perfect introduction to a unit on rhyming that will echo throughout the school year.

Cross-Curricular Connections

Connecting with math, you might make class graphs displaying favorite Mother Goose rhymes. If you work with number rhyming and jump-rope rhymes, students will be reading number words. Also, there is a natural crossover into music; each time you sing a song of any kind, you can emphasize the rhyming aspects.

To Start the Unit

Look at the suggested lessons and select those that are appropriate for your class. Read *A-Hunting We Will Go* aloud to your students, then proceed with any lesson you choose.

Literature Connections

Following is a list of books on the unit's focus for your students to read independently during the unit and even after you have finished the unit. If each student is reading a different book, discussions and activities regarding the unit's focus will be far richer than if everyone reads the same selection. See technique 1, Free Reading with Literature Connections, for suggestions.

Books

Aardema, Verna. 1981. *Bringing the Rain to Kapiti Plain*. Dial.

Aylesworth, Jim. 1990. *The Completed Hickory Dickory Dock*. Atheneum.

Barracca, Debra. 1990. *The Adventures of Taxi Dog*. Dial.

Bemelmans, Ludwig. 1977. *Madeline*. Puffin.

Clifton, Lucille. 1970. *Some of the Days of Everett Anderson*. Holt, Rinehart & Winston.

Dragonwagon, Crescent. 1989. *This Is the Bread I Baked for Ned*. Macmillan.

Fleming, Denise. 1991. *In the Tall, Tall Grass*. Henry Holt.

Fox, Mem. 1990. *Shoes from Grandpa*. Orchard.

Galdone, Paul. 1989. *Over in the Meadow*. S and S Trade.

Grossman, Bill. 1989. *Tommy at the Grocery Store*. Harper.

Hayes, Sarah. 1986. *This Is the Bear*. J. B. Lippincott.

Hennessy, B. G. 1990. *Jake Baked the Cake*. Viking.

Komalko, Leah. 1992. *Aunt Elaine Does the Dance from Spain*. Doubleday.

Lindbergh, Reeve. 1990. *The Day the Goose Got Loose*. Dial.

Martin, Bill. 1985. *Here Are My Hands*. Henry Holt.

Marzollo, Jean. 1981. *Uproar on Holler Cat Hill*. Dial.

Nerlove, Miriam. 1985. *I Made a Mistake*. Atheneum.

*Prelutsky, Jack, ed. 1983. *The Random House Book of Poetry*. New York: Random House.

*———. 1986. *Read-Aloud Rhymes for the Very Young*. New York: Alfred A. Knopf.

Rounds, Glen. 1990. *I Know an Old Lady Who Swallowed a Fly*. Holiday House.

Sendak, Maurice. 1962. *Pierre: A Cautionary Tale*. Harper.

Seuss, Dr. 1957. *The Cat in the Hat*. Random.

Shannon, George. 1981. *Piney Woods Peddler*. Greenwillow.

Shaw, Nancy. 1989. *Sheep on a Ship*. Houghton Mifflin.

Siebert, Diane. 1990. *Train Song*. Crowell.

Slepian, Jan. 1988. *The Hungry Thing*. Scholastic.

Smith, William Jay. 1989. *Ho for a Hat!* Little, Brown.

Taylor, Scott. 1990. *Dinosaur James*. Morrow.

Van Laan, Nancy. 1990. *Possum Come a-Knockin'*. Knopf.

Wilson, Sarah. 1991. *Garage Song*. Simon & Schuster.

Wing, Natasha. 1994. *Hippity Hop Frog on Top*. Simon & Schuster.

Winthrop, Elizabeth. 1986. *Shoes*. Harper.

Yektal, Nikl. 1987. *Bears in Pairs*. Bradbury.

Lesson 1

FREE READING WITH LITERATURE CONNECTIONS

Materials

books from the literature connections list or any other books that are structured around rhyming

Preparation

Gather books whose format is based on rhyming (see Literature Connections, page 32, for suggestions).

Procedure

Have students read freely in self-directed books for an extended period each day. They will also engage in some form of reporting their reading to the class. See technique 1, Free Reading with Literature Connections, for details.

More Challenge

After a week or so, students might select one rhyming book for which they could write another verse or chapter. They could do this activity individually or in groups of students who like the same book.

Multiple Intelligence Connections

Lesson 2

FAVORITE READ-ALOUDS

Materials

read-aloud books from literature connections or other books that are structured around rhymes

Preparation

Photocopy the cover or title page, whichever has a more interesting picture, of each day's read-aloud selection.

Procedure

Each day read aloud to your class one story from your unit-oriented collection. After about a week, have students vote on their favorite book. See technique 2, Read-Alouds, for details.

Multiple Intelligence Connections

Lesson 3

LEARN MOTHER GOOSE AND OTHER RHYMES

Materials

books and big books that have illustrated versions of Mother Goose and other good rhymes

Preparation

Find good versions of traditional and delightful new rhymes. Another option would be to create and duplicate simple illustrated versions of special poems to give to students to memorize.

Procedure

Step 1: Read poems and rhyming books to students often, and when you do, pause just before the second rhyming word and let students supply it.

Step 2: Have lots of rhyming books available for free reading time, and encourage students to recite as much of the familiar poems as they remember.

Step 3: Choose a poem each week or two to post in your room and recite with your students until many students have committed it to memory.

Step 4: Give a bonus to any child who can recite a poem all the way through (perhaps at recess or free play time). The bonus could be a copy of an illustrated version of the memorized poem that the child could color and keep.

Multiple Intelligence Connections

SIGNING TO POEMS

Materials

a book of sign language

Preparation

Learn the signs to accompany one nursery rhyme. Read technique 6, Sign Language, page 276.

Procedure

Step 1: Model the signs for the nursery rhyme. Let students practice with you until they have memorized the poem and the signs. The signs will help them memorize the poem, so do both at once.

Step 2: Introduce and teach more rhymes. Practice throughout the day.

More Challenge

Continue to learn signs during the year to accompany favorite songs and poems.

Multiple Intelligence Connections

Lesson 5

POEM OF THE WEEK

Material

collection of short, delightful poems printed on chart paper or on sentence strips

copies of those same poems on parent note 2-1

Preparation

First, find your poems (see suggestions below). Print one (or two) each week onto a chart or sentence strips for use with a pocket chart. For the first week, duplicate parent note 2-1 or 2-2 to send home with each student. In the following weeks, use parent note 2-3. Also prepare a clipboard with a class list to keep track of recitations.

Procedure

Step 1: Select one poem each week for your students to memorize. Pick poems that are upbeat and amusing; begin with very short poems. Print the poem on chart paper or sentence strips for a pocket chart; be sure to include the title and the author.

Step 2: Each Monday, post the new poem of the week. Read it to the class and let them read along with you several times during the day. At first, use a pointer to touch each word as it is recited; soon student volunteers can do this job. If you set a firm rule that each word is to be said only when the pointer touches it, students will soon learn to match the words they are memorizing with the words they are seeing.

Step 3: Monday, at the end of the day, send home parent note 2-1 with the poem of your choice.

Step 4: For the rest of the week, spend about 10 minutes a day helping students learn and recite the poem. The following system works well for me:

Have the whole class read the poem once or twice as a volunteer points to the words.

Ask one student volunteer to recite, either alone or with one or two friends.

I tell the reciters to stand facing the class so that the rest of the students can see the poem but the students who are reciting cannot. Thus, whenever the reciters are stumped, I snap my fingers and the whole class reads the missing word.

As each student recites I make a check on my class list, and sometimes a comment about the quality of recitation. My rule is that students can recite each poem only once, so that all students who wish to recite can have a turn and so that reciting will not last too long each day.

Another option is to let the rest of the students do a related task at their desks so that they do not become restless during the six to eight recitations each day. You may have students draw something about the poem in their own poetry books (see lesson 6: Personal Poetry Books). Or you might cover several words in the poem with self-stick notes and ask students to write the covered words, which will be revealed when the recitation time is finished. Or you might ask students to paste their copies of the poem into their poem books.

More Challenge

Select two poems each week, one short (4 to 8 lines long) and one longer and more complex. Reciting students can choose the one they wish to recite, and each student may choose to recite twice each week. Use parent note 2-2 if you decide on this plan.

Multiple Intelligence Connections

Lesson 6

PERSONAL POETRY BOOKS

Prerequisite

Do lesson 5.

Materials

pencils

crayons

teacher-made books

duplicates of the poem of the week

Preparation

Make a book with ten to fifteen pages of story paper (blank at the top and lined at the bottom). See technique 5, Teacher-Made Books. Also make a copy of the poem of the week for each student.

Procedure

Step 1: On Wednesday of each week that you do lesson 5 with your class, give students a teacher-made book and a copy of the poem of the week.

Step 2: Have students track (point to each word) as you all recite the poem aloud. Then show them how to paste the poem on the bottom half of the first page of their books and draw a picture to illustrate the poem on the top half.

Step 3: While students are drawing their pictures, volunteers may recite the poem.

Step 4: Each week students add another poem (or two) to their personal poetry books.

Step 5: Once a week, invite students to get together with a study partner and read all of the poems in their books to each other. Insist that students track as they read, thus linking words they memorize with the words they see. This activity keeps the poems fresh in the students' minds and is a wonderful beginning reading practice at which all students can be successful.

Step 6: Send these personal poetry books home at the end of each quarter so that students can read them to their parents and add them to home libraries.

More Challenge

■ If you are learning two poems each week, let students choose whether they want only one or both poems in their Personal Poetry Books. You may also offer to let students copy and illustrate favorite poems into their books. I have a free-time station where Mother Goose poems are printed onto cards for students to copy as they wish.

- Students who enjoy printing may prefer to copy the poems of the week into their books in their own handwriting. It provides an excellent and meaningful opportunity for handwriting practice.

Multiple Intelligence Connections

POETRY SEQUENCING

Materials

charts or sentence strips from previous poems of the week

Preparation

As you come to the close of each week, remove the poem of the week from the board or pocket chart. If it has been on a chart, cut it up so that each line is on a separate strip of paper. If the poem is on sentence strips, save them as is. Keep the strips of each poem together with the title and author strip and secure all with a large paper clip.

Note: After three weeks of doing a poem of the week (lesson 5), you can do this exercise with a group of six students, perhaps during reading-group time. After a longer time, depending on whether you are learning one or two poems each week, you can do this exercise with the whole class at once.

Procedure

Step 1: Divide your group into partners and give each pair one of the poems with the mixed strips.

Step 2: Students must work together on the floor or at a table to arrange the poem in the correct order with the title and author at the top.

Step 3: When students think their poem is in the correct order, they must read it softly aloud, touching each word as they recite. At this point, students will often find that they need to move some of the strips.

Step 4: After both students have read the poem in the correct order, they raise their hands and read it to you.

Step 5: If their sequence is correct, exchange the strips for another poem. Continue for about ten minutes and allow each set of partners to sequence and read at least three different poems.

Multiple Intelligence Connections

Lesson 8

SINGING RHYME SONGS

Materials

a good rhyming song

Preparation

Find a good rhyming song. To select a song to teach children how to rhyme, I rely on a particular kind of rhyming song that invites students to invent and fill in the final rhyming word. For example, "Tiger, tiger, dressed in red,/Went to the jungle to make his _____," "Down by the Bay," and "Willaby, Wallaby" are excellent for this activity.

Procedure

Sing the song with students, pausing for them to insert rhyming words. In second grade, you might ask all students to write down each rhyming word they are thinking of before anyone is allowed to say or sing it. Sing this type of song several times a week during the school year. This activity can provide a novel way to excuse students one at a time to lunch or recess.

Multiple Intelligence Connections

WRITE A SONG

Materials

chart paper and materials for making a class big book

felt-tip pens

optional: instruments: piano, guitar, autoharp

optional: teacher-made books for song books

Preparation

Find and teach the class several songs with a rhyming pattern such as those listed below. If you want students to write and illustrate the song in their own books, make each student a book (see technique 5, Teacher-Made Books, page 273).

Procedure

Step 1: Choose a familiar song or jump-rope chant to which students can write their own verses. Some examples are *A-Hunting We Will Go; The Ants Go Marching One by One; Hey, Li-lee, li-lee, li-lee; Teddy Bear, Teddy Bear, Turn Around;* and *Down by the Bay.*

Step 2: Add a new line to the song, then have students help you make a rhyme list for the last word of their new line. For example, if you choose "I know a boy whose name is Andy" for "Hey, Li-lee," then brainstorm a list of words that rhyme with *Andy* and will fit at the end of the next line: *candy, sandy, handy, Mandy.*

Step 3: Students work together to think of a second line that would work, such as "He went to the beach and got all sandy," or "If you need a friend, he's really handy." Record each new verse on a permanent chart or in the pages of the class book.

Step 4: Sing the verses that you create, adding musical accompaniment, or jump rope to them.

More Challenge

Students write individual song books.

Step 1: As the class writes each verse from the brainstormed lists, students copy it into their teacher-made books and illustrate it. Students might all write what the class decides on, or each student could write a verse of his or her own.

Step 2: When books are complete, students pair up and read them to one another. Every new reading partner can sign the backs of the other students' books after the authors have read it aloud.

Step 3: Before taking the books home, students can choose the pages that they think they did best. Photocopy this page and add it to the students' portfolios.

Note: For beginning writers, you might prefer to make the books with copy paper on which you have already printed and duplicated the basic words to the chorus and part of each verse of the song, leaving blanks where the new words will go.

Multiple Intelligence Connections

JUMP-ROPE RHYMES

Materials

a long jump rope
jump-rope rhymes

Preparation

Get a long jump rope and learn some jump-rope rhymes. You will find many in *A Rocket in My Pocket*.

Procedure

Step 1: Add a jump-rope station to your P.E. line-up. Have two students turn the rope for the jumper.

Step 2: Each week as students are jumping and others are waiting their turns, teach a new jump-rope song. This practice will add to their rhyming repertoire. These rhymes may be used in lesson 9.

Multiple Intelligence Connections

Unit
2

MATERIALS

Parent Note 2-1

*Use this note as an introduction if you are going to send home **one poem each week**. Attach the first week's poem to the bottom of the note before duplicating.*

Dear Parent,

This year I am going to ask each student to memorize one poem each week. In addition to helping your child learn how to read, this poetry assignment will also increase your child's brain power. I hope you will help with this weekly project.

Each Monday I will send a new poem home and your child will have the rest of the week to learn it. If you post the poem on a refrigerator or a bulletin board and say it together several times each day, your child will soon have the poem memorized. Once your child has memorized the poem, you can help further by asking him or her to point to each word of the poem as it is recited. This tracking helps children learn to read as the memorized words are matched with those that are seen.

The first poem is below. I hope that you and your child enjoy this part of our curriculum this year.

Sincerely,

Developing Intelligences through Literature © 1996 Zephyr Press, Tucson, AZ

Parent Note 2-2

Dear Parent,

This year I am going to ask each student to memorize at least one poem each week. In addition to helping your child learn how to read, this poetry assignment will also strengthen brain power. I hope you will help with this weekly project.

Each Monday, I will send two poems home with your child and he or she will have the rest of the week to memorize them. Only one is required, but if your child likes extra challenge, go for both. If you post the poems on a refrigerator or a bulletin board and say one together several times each day, your child will soon have the poems memorized. Once your child has memorized a poem, you could help further by asking him or her to point to each word of the poem as it is recited. This tracking helps children learn to read as words that are memorized are matched with words that are seen.

The first poems are below. I hope that you and your child enjoy this part of our curriculum this year.

Sincerely,

Parent Note 2-3

Choose either of the following notes to accompany poems after the first week depending on whether you are sending one poem or two poems each week. Attach the week's poems before duplicating the letters.

Dear Parent,

Here is this week's poem for your child to memorize. Thank you for your help in this homework; the students are doing an excellent job of reciting the poems in class. I hope you will be able to continue to help as your child memorizes this poem this week.

Thank you.

Dear Parent,

Here are this week's poems for your child to memorize. Thank you for your help in this homework. The students are doing an excellent job of reciting the poems in class. I hope you will be able to continue to help as your child memorizes one or both of these poems this week.

Thank you.

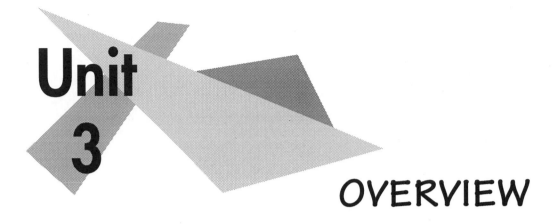

Unit 3

OVERVIEW

Central Literature Selection:
Jaime O'Rourke and the Big Potato
by Tomie DePaola

Unit Focus: Solving Problems Together
Grades: K–3

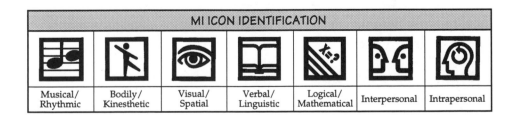

THINKING SKILLS SYMBOLS IDENTIFICATION				
Personal Connection	Creation	Mastery	Reasoning	Metacognition

MI ICON IDENTIFICATION						
Musical/ Rhythmic	Bodily/ Kinesthetic	Visual/ Spatial	Verbal/ Linguistic	Logical/ Mathematical	Interpersonal	Intrapersonal

Lesson 1: **Free Reading with Literature Connections** (Grades 1–3; twenty minutes a day)

Students read books of their own choosing, selected from books that address the unit topic.

Lesson 2: **Favorite Read-Alouds** (Grades K–3; five to ten minutes a day)

Students keep track of all read-alouds that match the unit's focus and vote on their favorites.

Lesson 3: **Solving Problems Together** (Grades K–3; one class period)

Students discuss and draw the three stages of a problem that they have solved with someone's help.

Lesson 4: **Lifting Heavy Objects** (Grades K–3; one class period)

Partners work with heavy objects and rulers to try to solve the problem of how a fulcrum works.

Lesson 5: **Transporting Heavy Objects** (Grades K–3; one class period)

Using a large, heavy object and some doweling or broomsticks, the whole class works together to solve the problem of how ancient peoples transported heavy objects, such as pyramid blocks, over long distances.

Lesson 6: **Problem-Solving Homework** (Grades 2–3; one or more class periods)

With their parents' assistance and using ordinary objects found around their homes, students try to create a simple cart with axles and wheels that turn.

Lesson 7: **Potatoes, Potatoes** (Grades 1–3; one class period plus follow-up)

Remembering the villagers' second problem, that is, getting sick of eating potatoes, students brainstorm and interview family members to list many different ways to cook potatoes. Then they cook several recipes they have never tried.

Lesson 8: **A Musical Problem** (Grades K–3; two class periods)

Students create an Irish Dance.

Lesson 9: **Solving a School Problem** (Grades 1–3; one class period plus follow-up)

You choose a genuine school problem and challenge students to work together to solve it.

Lesson 10: **Cooperative Problem-Solving Lessons** (Grades K–3; one class period each)

Four lessons teach students how to work together to solve problems. Although based on cooperative learning techniques, these lessons can be done with or without the social skills training.

Lesson 10A: **Cross the River** (Grades K–3)

Partners use building materials to construct a bridge across a river.

Lesson 10B: **Find the Pattern** (Grades 1–3)

Partners work together to solve a series of number patterns.

Lesson 10C: **Menu Problems** (Grade 1)

Partners solve problems about money and a menu.

Lesson 10D: **Candy Store Problems** (Grades 2–3)

Partners solve easier problems dealing with penny candy prices.

Lesson 11: **Sequencing on the Wall** (Grades 1–3; one long class period)

Students retell, illustrate, and sequence the central story to put on a bulletin board.

Synopsis of Jaime O'Rourke and the Big Potato

Tomie DePaola's rendition of an Irish folk tale is about a lazy farmer who captures a leprechaun. Instead of a pot of gold, Jaime O'Rourke settles for a magic potato seed that grows a gigantic potato. It grows so big that it blocks the only road in and out of town. Community cooperation solves the problem, and Jaime is promised a life of plenty if he will not plant any more of his magic potato seeds.

Explanation of Unit Focus: Solving Problems Together

Students will think about how to work with other people as they read other books and solve problems with their classmates.

Cross-Curricular Connections

This unit is an excellent introduction to the use of cooperative learning in your classroom. It will also work well with any wise-choices health programs that you may have, such as home fire safety, drugs and alcohol, dangers from strangers, emergencies and first aid, bullies, and many other difficulties.

The fulcrum in the story can add to a unit on simple machines, all of which were invented to solve problems. Another connection will be with any program that teaches children how to deal with problems that come up at school, either academic or social.

To Start the Unit

Look at the suggested lessons and select those that are appropriate for your class. Read *Jaime O'Rourke and the Big Potato* aloud to your students, then proceed with any lesson you choose.

Literature Connections

Following is a list of books on the unit's focus for your students to read independently during the unit and even after you have finished the unit. If each student is reading a different book, discussions and activities regarding the unit's focus will be far richer than if everyone reads the same selection. See technique 1, Free Reading with Literature Connections, for suggestions.

Picture Books

Bodecker, N. M. 1974. *Mushroom Center Disaster*. Atheneum.

Brown, Marcia. 1974. *Stone Soup*. Macmillan.

Chapman, Carol. 1981. *Herbie's Troubles*. Dutton.

Choi, Sook Nyul. 1993. *Halmoni and the Picnic*. Houghton Mifflin.

Cohen, Miriam. 1978. *Bee My Valentine*. Greenwillow.

Douglass, Barbara. 1982. *Good as New*. Lothrop.

Friedman, Ina R. 1984. *How My Parents Learned to Eat*. Houghton Mifflin.

Hoban, Russell. 1969. *Best Friends for Frances*. Harper.

Hughes, Shirley. 1984. *An Evening at Alfie's*. Lothrop.

Jones, Chuck. 1986. *William the Backwards Skunk*. Crown.

Keats, Ezra. 1981. *Regards to the Man in the Moon*. Four Winds.

Lionni, Leo. 1963. *Swimmy*. Knopf.

Lord, John Vernon. 1990. *Giant Jam Sandwich*. Houghton Mifflin.

McKissack, Patricia. 1989. *Nettie Jo's Friends*. Knopf.

Morgan, Pierr. 1990. *The Turnip*. Philomel.

Ransome, Arthur. 1968. *The Fool of the World and the Flying Ship*. Farrar, Straus and Giroux.

Rayner, Mary. 1976. *Mr. and Mrs. Pig's Evening Out*. Macmillan.

Wescott, Nadine B. 1981. *Giant Vegetable Garden*. Little.

Wilson, Sarah. 1989. *Muskrat, Muskrat, Eat Your Peas*. Simon & Schuster.

Young, Ed. 1989. *Lon Po Po*. Philomel.

Longer Books

Bridgers, Sue. 1979. *All Together Now*. Knopf.

Foote, Timothy. 1980. *The Great Ringtail Garbage Caper*. Houghton Mifflin.

Hamilton, Virginia. 1984. *House of Dies Drear*. Macmillan.

King-Smith, Dick. 1980. *Pigs Might Fly*. Viking.

Langton, Jane. 1980. *Fragile Flag*. Viking.

Merrill, Jean. 1964. *The Pushcart War*. Scott.

Nesbit, E. 1991. *Railway Children*. Puffin.

O'Brien, Robert C. 1971. *Mr. Frisby and the Rats of NIMH*. Atheneum.

Pascal, Francine. 1980. *Hand-Me-Down-Kid*. Viking.

Phipson, Joan. 1978. *When the City Stopped*. Atheneum.

Robert, Willo Davis. 1980. *Girl with the Silver Eyes*. Atheneum.

Sachs, Marilyn. 1969. *Peter and Veronica*. Scholastic.

Selden, George. 1960. *Cricket in Times Square*. Farrar, Straus and Giroux.

Snyder, Silpha Keatley. 1979. *Famous Stanley Kidnapping Case*. Atheneum.

Treadgold, Mary. 1978. *We Couldn't Leave Dinah*. Jonathan Cape.

Turkle, Brinton. 1970. *Mooncoin Castle*. Viking.

Van Leeuwen, Jean. 1982. *Great Rescue Operation*. Dial.

Warner, Gertrude. 1942. *Boxcar Children*. Whitman.

White, E. B. 1952. *Charlotte's Web*. Harper.

Wrightson, Patricia. 1968. *A Racecourse for Andy*. Harcourt.

FREE READING WITH LITERATURE CONNECTIONS

Materials

books from the literature connections list or any other books about solving problems together

Preparation

Gather a variety of books of different lengths and different reading levels that address the unit focus (see Literature Connections, page 53, for suggestions).

Procedure

Have students read freely in self-selected books for an extended period each day. Also have them engage in some form of reporting their reading to the class. (See technique 1, Free Reading with Literature Connections, on page 267 for details.)

Multiple Intelligence Connections

FAVORITE READ-ALOUDS

Materials

read-aloud books from literature connections or other books about solving problems together

Preparation

Photocopy the cover or title page, whichever has a more interesting picture, of each day's read-aloud selection.

Procedure

Read aloud to your class at least one story a day from your unit-oriented collection. After about a week, students will vote on their favorites. (See technique 2, Read-Alouds, on page 268 for details.)

Multiple Intelligence Connections

 **Lesson 3**

SOLVING PROBLEMS TOGETHER

Materials

12-by-18-inch white art paper

crayons or felt-tip pens

pencils

Preparation

Cut the white construction paper in half lengthwise. Cut another colored construction paper sheet for the cover of the class book. You may want to laminate the colored cover.

Procedure

Step 1: Read or reread *Jaime O'Rourke and the Big Potato.*

Step 2: Have a class discussion about problems that people run into every day (forget your lunch, miss the bus, can't find your shoes, run out of milk for cereal).

Step 3: Ask students to help you list problems that they have experienced and the solutions that someone has helped them come up with (see example on page 57).

Problem	Solution
couldn't find my shoes	Brother found them under my bed.
missed the bus	Mom drove me to school.
forgot my lunch money	Miss Allen let me charge for a day.
fell in a puddle	Borrowed extra clothes from the office.
got a flat tire on my bike	Joey helped me change it.

Step 4: Ask students to choose one of the problems from the list and draw a *before* and an *after* picture in the following manner:

Students fold drawing paper lengthwise into thirds.

In the first third, students draw the problem.

In the last third, students draw the solution.

In the middle third, students draw the person or people who helped solve the problem.

Additional Step for Grades 1 through 3

- Students write a sentence for each section of the picture. Be sure that spelling and punctuation are correct, as these will be read by other students.

- Students can show or read their finished products to several other children.

- Collect all the drawings and bind them into a class book called *Solving Problems Together*. Read the book to the class and add it to your class library.

Multiple Intelligence Connections

LIFTING HEAVY OBJECTS

Materials

rulers

felt-tip pens

some moderately heavy objects

Preparation

Gather moderately heavy objects (a number 2 can of beans, a tape dispenser, a flat rock, a thick pocket book, and so on) that students can lift using a fulcrum and a ruler.

Procedure

Step 1: Read *Jaime O'Rourke and the Big Potato* to your class.

Step 2: Talk to students about how people through the ages have solved the problem of lifting heavy items. Ask them to tell you some of the machines that people currently use to lift heavy items, and list these ideas on a chalkboard or chart paper. Read the list aloud together.

Step 3: Ask students to think back to the days before we had these machines. Ask them to think of several ways people moved heavy objects. Ask them to imagine a rock as big as the teacher's desk, so heavy that all of them together could not move it. What could move such a heavy rock? What did the townsfolk try in *Jaime O'Rourke and the Big Potato?*

Step 4: Tell students that they are going to work with partners to experiment lifting a heavy object using a fulcrum and a lever. Ask them to tell you how they think a fulcrum works.

Step 5: Show students how to place the felt-tip pen or other dowel-like shape (the fulcrum) under the ruler (the lever) and to place the lever under the heavy object. Do not show them how to lift the heavy object. Tell them to try putting their pens in different places along the lengths of the rulers, to use only their little fingers to push down the ends of the rulers that are opposite the objects, and to notice what happens (see figure 3-1). Using their little fingers only will give the children a better feel for when the object becomes easier to move.

Figure 3-1. Using a pen as a fulcrum

Step 6: Give students 10 minutes to take turns trying to lift the various objects. Circulate and help them understand how to move the fulcrum (felt-tip pen) to various positions along the length of the ruler.

Step 7: Discuss results with the class and let students demonstrate any rules that they discovered, such as "the closer the fulcrum is to the object, the easier it is to lift."

Step 8: Ask students to draw a picture each of the easiest way to use a lever and a fulcrum to lift a heavy weight. Ask students to label the lever, the fulcrum, and the heavy object they chose to draw.

Adaptations for Kindergarten and Early First Grade

- Draw pictures with or instead of the list in step 2.

- Work with groups of five or six children at a time to do the experiments.

More Challenge

Ask students to write on the backs of their papers why they think the object seems lighter when the fulcrum is close to it.

Multiple Intelligence Connections

Lesson 5
TRANSPORTING HEAVY OBJECTS

Materials

a heavy object, such as a suitcase filled with magazines or a box filled with books

6 round sticks (dowels or broom handles) that are at least as long as the heavy object is wide

Preparation

Obtain the heavy object and the six round sticks. This lesson is not dependent upon lesson 4, but they go well together.

Procedure

Step 1: Ask what kinds of things people in ancient Egypt and South America may have used to move trees, boats, rocks, statues, or blocks for building the pyramids.

Step 2: Clear a path from where your heavy object is sitting to the opposite side of the room, or do this activity outside on the pavement. Ask students to help you figure out how to use the dowels to move the heavy object from one side of the room to the other. Remind them how the townspeople helped Jaime O'Rourke and encourage students to help each other think.

Step 3: Accept and try any reasonable suggestions. You will eventually find out that pushing the object up onto one crosswise dowel, then onto another, and another will get it rolling. When one dowel pops out behind the object it can be placed in the front.

Step 4: Let a team of six students each place one dowel at the front of the heavy object and then go around to the back to get it when it moves out and put it back at the front once again. They should do so as quickly as they can. This effort takes teamwork. If students are having trouble identifying which dowel is theirs, ask them to figure out a solution. (Coloring the end of each dowel with a different color pen is one possibility.) Let several different teams have a turn.

Step 5: Tell students that they have just discovered what many scientists believe is the way in which ancient peoples moved blocks for the pyramids and rocks for the giant statues on Easter Island.

Additional Steps for Grades 2 and 3

■ Let a team of six students each place one dowel at the front of the heavy object and then go around to the back to get it when it moves out and put it back at the front once again. They should do so as quickly as they can. This effort takes teamwork. If students are having trouble identifying which dowel is theirs, ask them to figure out a solution. (Coloring the end of each dowel with a different color pen is one possibility.) Let several different teams have a turn.

Optional Step

Give all students round toothpicks and a new rectangular eraser and challenge them to move the eraser across their desktops using the toothpicks as rollers. If students do the work in pairs, they may keep track of how many times they had to replace the toothpicks to move the eraser from one side of the desk to the other.

More Challenge

Step 1: Students try to figure out how the use of wheels made this system obsolete. Show students an inexpensive toy car on which they can clearly see the axle. Ask them what the difference is between this axle-and-wheel structure and the dowels, and which is more convenient.

Step 2: Have students work in small groups with your assistance to try to figure out how the dowels could have been turned into the first wheels. (If the center sections of the dowels were whittled down, the dowel would serve as an axle with attached wheels. Or if larger wooden circles were attached to the ends of one of the dowels, the result would be an axle and wheels. But then how are the wheels attached to the heavy object?)

Step 3: Ask for students' ideas and challenge them to look at their toys and return to tell you the next day, or do lesson 6.

Multiple Intelligence Connections

PROBLEM-SOLVING HOMEWORK

Materials

a copy of parent note 3-1

sheet of story paper for each student

extra materials (toothpick, carrot slices, and marshmallows or a lump of modeling clay) for students who may not have the opportunity to do the work at home

Preparation

Photocopy parent note 3-1, one for each student. Gather materials to help students who can't usually complete their homework at home.

Procedure

Step 1: Give students copies of parent note 3-1 and go over it with them.

Step 2: The following day, let any students who could not do their homework build a vehicle with materials that you provide for them.

Step 3: After all students have created a wheeled vehicle, divide the class into groups of six.

Step 4: Send the groups to the corners of the room for privacy, and ask students to show their vehicles to their groups and tell how they solved the problem of attaching wheels that turn. Some students may use these ideas to revise their home-built products.

Step 5: When all have shared, give students a sheet of story paper with room for both pictures and writing. Tell students to return to their desks to draw pictures of their vehicle and write explanations of their thinking process when they were building. Ask them to tell you what they tried and how they finally figured out what to do to successfully attach the wheels to the vehicle in a way that the wheels turned (see figure 3-2).

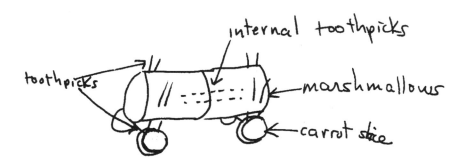

Figure 3-2. A marshmallow car

Multiple Intelligence Connections

Lesson 7
POTATOES, POTATOES

Materials

paper for each student

pencils for each student

class graph

supplies for cooking some potato recipes (optional)

Procedure

Step 1: Read *Jaime O'Rourke and the Big Potato* to your class.

Step 2: Ask students to try to remember the second big problem in the book (people were tired of eating potatoes).

Step 3: Tell students that they are going to help solve this problem by finding out how many different ways potatoes can be prepared. Start a brainstorming list in the classroom, and then give students a homework assignment to ask parents how many ways they can think of to prepare potatoes. Students may write "How many ways do you know to prepare potatoes?" on a sheet of paper and come back with a list of parents' answers.

Step 4: The next day, have students share their lists with partners and star any answers that are the same. This step allows each child to talk, listen, and explain his or her ideas.

Step 5: Add all ideas to the class list. Remind students of the original problem that led to this great variety.

Step 6: Ask each child to pick a favorite way to prepare potatoes and make a class graph based on the answers.

Optional Step 7: Find recipes that students have never tried and cook some at school. Record favorites on another graph.

Multiple Intelligence Connections

Lesson 8

A MUSICAL PROBLEM

Materials

recordings of various Irish songs, with or without lyrics

Preparation

Gather recordings of Irish songs.

Procedure

Step 1: Play songs for students. If you find songs with words, you may add the song charts as described in technique 3, Music Connections, page 270, and students may learn to sing them.

Step 2: Have students select one of the songs that they think would make the best dance. They must all agree on one song.

Step 3: Select a student to be your partner and model how two people work together to create dance steps. Model enough so students see some possible dance steps and understand how to negotiate with each other.

Step 4: Pair students, and have each set of partners create a dance to go with the music. While students work on their dances, play the song several times.

Step 5: When students have their dances ready, play the song while all students dance.

Optional Step 6: Ask for volunteers to perform for the class. Let three or four couples perform together to lessen pressure and reduce time spent on this activity.

Multiple Intelligence Connections

SOLVING A SCHOOL PROBLEM

Materials

paper for each student

pencils for each student

supplies for the problem the class decides to solve

Preparation

Talk to the administration about a school-wide problem that your students might help to solve. Get permission to solve it.

Procedure

Step 1: Read *Jaime O'Rourke and the Big Potato* to your class.

Step 2: Tell students that you would like their help solving a real problem at your school. This problem must be a genuine problem and one that your students can actually help solve. Your students might choose one of the following:

> *no system for recycling papers*
>
> *no swing set and no money in budget for one*
>
> *candy wrappers all over the playground*
>
> *no orientation for new students*

Step 3: Ask students to write down any solutions they can imagine for the problem. Then make a class list of their ideas. Discuss them, and vote on those that are feasible.

Step 4: Make a plan to implement your solution and proceed.

Step 5: Ask students to write notes to their parents explaining how they helped to solve the school problem. If parents helped with the solution, include an expression of appreciation.

Note: You may also do this activity to solve classroom problems, such as too much paper on the floor at the end of the day or a long line and delay in washing hands before lunch.

Multiple Intelligence Connections

Lesson 10

COOPERATIVE PROBLEM-SOLVING LESSONS

These lessons are not literature-based, but they are linked to the focus of the unit: solving problems together. I have included them especially for teachers who use cooperative learning in their classrooms. This unit of study is an excellent introduction to cooperative learning because it emphasizes the importance of people working together to solve problems that one person cannot solve as well alone.

Use the following problem-solving lessons in your classroom whether or not you are schooled in the cooperative learning strategies. I have divided the lessons into two sections, one without the formal cooperative learning aspect and one with it. In either case, your students will be involved in working together to solve problems in the lessons that follow.

Note: If you would like to read more about cooperative learning, the following books will help you start:

Cooperative Learning, Spencer Kagan, Kagan Cooperative Learning, San Juan Capistrano, CA, 1992.

Cooperative Learning Lessons for Little Ones, Lorna Curran, Resources for Teachers, San Juan Capistrano, CA, 1990.

Cooperative Learning: The Magazine for Cooperation in Education, International Association for the Study of Cooperation in Education, Santa Cruz, CA.

Lesson 10 A

CROSS THE RIVER

Materials

a construction-paper river

assorted building materials, such as building blocks or Legos, that a kindergarten classroom might have for free play

Preparation

Cut and connect blue construction paper to represent a river about one foot wide and twenty feet long to lay on your classroom floor. Gather materials that students can use to build a bridge over the small river. If building materials are not available in your classroom, you can use toothpicks and little balls of modeling clay or miniature marshmallows.

Procedure

Step 1: Show students the river you have made and tell them to imagine that they are little people who need to cross that river. Ask them to work together to build a structure that can get the little people safely from one side to the other without touching the "water."

Step 2: Divide the class into groups and give each group enough building materials to build a bridge over the water. Remind students that the little people will need steps up to the bridge.

Step 3: Circulate and help students formulate their suggestions and try them out.

Step 4: When all groups have succeeded, ask one person from each group to share the group's ideas and success with the rest of the class.

Optional Step 5: Students return to their seats to draw pictures of their bridges and write about what helped them figure out how to get across the water. For kindergarten the teacher can write what the students dictate.

Additional Steps for Cooperative Learning Goals

- Set making suggestions as a social skill. Model by showing students how they might say, "I have an idea . . . " or "I know what we could try . . . "

- Circulate as students are working. You will be helping and guiding the students to form ideas and try experiments; carry a clipboard to write down the suggestions you hear students make.

- At the end of the lesson, after students have shared their bridges, read the comments that you heard along with the names of the students who said them. This recognition increases the likelihood that students will use this discussion skill next time because they have been rewarded and because they have heard real-life examples.

Multiple Intelligence Connections

Lesson 10 B   FIND THE PATTERN

Materials

one copy of work sheet 3-1, Find the Pattern, for each pair of students

pencils

Preparation

Photocopy work sheet 3-1 for each pair of students in the class.

Procedure

Step 1: Divide the class into pairs and give one work sheet 3-1 to each pair of students.

Step 2: Do the first pattern for the class; show them how you notice and then extend the pattern.

Step 3: Let partners try to solve the rest together of the patterns together.

Step 4: After the solutions are discovered, let students share their answers aloud and check their own papers.

Step 5: Have students turn their papers over and take turns writing compliments to their partners about their helpfulness, for example, "Janet, it helped me when you would read the pattern out loud," or "Barry, I liked the way you didn't give up."

Additional Steps for Cooperative Learning Goals

- Set giving compliments as a social skill goal. Model this skill by saying, "That's a great idea," "Good thinking," or "Way to go, Katie."

- Circulate to write down compliments that you hear. When the lesson is over and the students have finished writing their final compliments, read aloud the ones you heard given during the lesson, along with the names of those students who gave them.

Multiple Intelligence Connections

Lesson 10 C MENU PROBLEMS

Materials

one overhead transparency made from work sheet 3-2 or 3-3, Rose's Restaurant, or a chart or poster based on that work sheet and posted on a bulletin board

paper

pencils

Preparation

Either make an overhead transparency of work sheet 3-2 or 3-3 or create and post a permanent chart based on Rose's menu or another that more closely matches the eating experiences and number wisdom of your students.

Procedure

Step 1: Show and discuss the menu, then divide your class into pairs and assign each pair a problem like those in the list below. Some problems may have more than one possible answer.

> *If you had $5.00, which sandwich, drink, and dessert could you afford?*
>
> *If you had $5.00, which two sandwiches could you buy and have $2.00 left for a milk shake?*
>
> *What is the most money you could spend for one sandwich, one drink, one side dish, and one dessert?*
>
> *What is the least amount of money you could spend for one sandwich, one drink, one side dish, and one dessert?*
>
> *What four different sandwiches could you buy for $6.00?*
>
> *What would your favorite four choices cost?*
>
> *If you had $10.00, what would you buy for you and your best friend?*

Step 2: Have students solve several problems in one session, or do this activity for ten to fifteen minutes every day for the duration of this unit or even beyond. This project is good to do for a brief time each day because it helps students work on their math skills and also gives them an opportunity to discuss and solve problems.

Step 3: If you continue to use this format for longer than the duration of the unit, make up other menus for greater variety. You might do menus for a candy store, a taco stand, a hamburger stand, a pizza place, a fried chicken restaurant, or a Chinese restaurant.

More Challenge

Step 1: Ask students to find at least two answers for each problem for which there are multiple answers.

Step 2: Ask students to make up a question like the ones you have asked and have them show at least one correct solution. Then have them pose their question to the class for the next day's problem.

Note: If you wish to change and fill in prices that are the right level of challenge for your students, use the second menu, work sheet 3-3.

Additional Steps for Cooperative Learning Goals

- Choose using quiet voices as a social skill. Model this by using your voice at the level you would like students to employ.

- While students are solving their problems, circulate and put stars on the papers of students who are using quiet voices. Then come back and give more stars repeatedly to keep the level of talking as low as you would like to have it.

Multiple Intelligence Connections

CANDY STORE PROBLEMS

Materials

one overhead transparency made from work sheet 3-4, Rose's Candy Store, or a chart or poster based on that work sheet and posted on a bulletin board

paper

pencils

Preparation

Make an overhead transparency of work sheet 3-4 or create and post a permanent chart based on that menu or another that more closely matches the eating experiences and number skills of your students.

Step 1: Show and discuss the menu, then divide your class into pairs and assign each pair a problem like those in the list below. Some problems may have more than one answer.

If you had five pennies, what could you buy?

If you had seven pennies, what could you buy?

If you had eight pennies and you bought a Tootsie Roll, what else could you buy?

If you bought six ribbon candies, how much would they cost?

If you bought two candy bars, how much change would you get from a quarter?

If you had fifty cents, what candy would you buy?

Step 2: After giving the students time to work on their problems, come together as a class and ask the pairs to tell how they solved their problems; recognize all of the different correct answers. You can do several problems in one session, then repeat the activity on several other occasions.

More Challenge

Follow the suggestions for more challenge in Lesson 10C.

Additional Steps for Cooperative Learning Goals

- Follow the suggestions at the end of lesson 10C; they are applicable to this lesson as well.

Multiple Intelligence Connections

Lesson 11

SEQUENCING ON THE WALL

Materials

pencils
crayons or felt-tip pens for each student
colored paper for bulletin board
story paper for each student
one sheet 12-by-18-inch art paper

Preparation

In large letters print the book's title and author's name on the art paper. Also have other materials ready to cover a bulletin board as described below.

Procedure

Step 1: Read or reread *Jaime O'Rourke and the Big Potato.* Then ask students to raise their hands to tell one thing that happened in the story (not necessarily in order).

Step 2: As each student raises a hand to tell you about another story event, hand that child a sheet of story paper and ask him or her to write a description of the event on the lined portion and illustrate it on the unlined half of the paper.

Step 3: Continue until all story elements are remembered and described by someone. You may have a number of students left over. Ask those students to help you prepare and decorate the bulletin board for the story when the other students have finished writing and illustrating.

Step 4: As students finish printing their bits of the story, check and correct any errors. If a student has made an error, challenge him or her to find it with a comment such as, "One word in this line needs a capital; which is it?" or "Which one of the words in this row is misspelled?" Do not mark the mistakes, but have students erase and correct them.

Step 5: When all students are finished writing and illustrating, ask which student thinks he or she has the story element that occurred first. When a student responds, ask the class to decide by vote if they agree or not.

Step 6: When the class agrees on the first story element, ask its author to pin it in the first position on the bulletin board. Continue adding one element at a time as the class votes.

Step 7: Read the whole story aloud to the class, pointing to each page as you read.

Step 8: In students' free time later, they can read the bulletin board by pointing to each word as they work their way across the wall.

Additional Step for First Grade

- Before each student goes off to work, you might print the student's sentence on a slip of scrap paper for the student to copy correctly.

Multiple Intelligence Connections

Unit 3

MATERIALS

Parent Note 3-1
Problem-Solving Homework

Dear Parent,

Our class has been studying problem solving. We read a book called *Jaime O'Rourke and the Big Potato* in which a whole village helped Jaime O'Rourke solve his problem of what to do with a gigantic potato.

Your child's homework tonight is to enlist your help (and the help of anyone else in the household who is willing) to solve the problem of how to build a vehicle with an axle and wheels that will turn. Please help your child figure out how to build a vehicle that has wheels that can turn.

The vehicle may be as small as a matchbox car. You may use anything that you have around the house: blocks, empty boxes, toothpicks, cardboard, vegetables, hard candy, clay, or other materials. If you happen to have expertise in working with wood, you could certainly use that as well. Do not be concerned about the appearance of the vehicle. Our emphasis is on the problem solving your child will do, particularly how to attach an axle and wheels to a wagon so that the wheels will turn.

Following is an idea your child can duplicate if nothing else comes to mind. Encourage him or her to figure out how to put it together by giving hints and encouragement.

Materials

four round carrot slices

two round toothpicks

marshmallows or a lump of modeling clay

Procedure

Step 1: Make wheels and axles by pushing the toothpicks through the carrot slices.

Step 2: Use the marshmallow (or a square of modeling clay) as the vehicle. Push two toothpicks down through the marshmallow on each of the four corners to form holders for the axles. The vehicle will not be fixed to the wheels, but it should roll on them.

Have your child bring the vehicle you create to school on _____ to share with the other students.

Thank you for your help.

Work Sheet 3-1
Find the Pattern

If you would like to add patterns that increase the challenge level for your class use the blanks at the bottom. If you don't want to add any, just cut off the bottom before you duplicate the work sheet.

A. 1, 2, 3, 4, ____ , ____ , ____ , ____ , ____ , ____ , ____ , ____ ,

B. 10, 9, 8, 7, ____ , ____ , ____ , ____ , ____ , ____ ,

C. 2, 4, 6, 8, ____ , ____ , ____ , ____ , ____ , ____ ,

D. A, B, C, D, E, ____ , ____ , ____ , ____ , ____ , ____ ,

E. 10, 20, 30, ____ , ____ , ____ , ____ , ____ , ____ ,

F. 1, 3, 5, 7, ____ , ____ , ____ , ____ , ____ , ____ ,

G. 1, 4, 7, 10, 13, 16, ____ , ____ , ____ , ____ , ____ , ____ ,

H. 5, 10, 15, 20, 25, ____ , ____ , ____ , ____ , ____ , ____ ,

I. A, C, E, G, I, K, ____ , ____ , ____ , ____ , ____ , ____ ,

J. 100, 200, 300, ____ , ____ , ____ , ____ , ____ , ____ ,

K. ____ , ____ , ____ , ____ , ____ , ____ , ____ , ____ , ____ ,

L. ____ , ____ , ____ , ____ , ____ , ____ , ____ , ____ , ____ , ____ ,

M. ____ , ____ , ____ , ____ , ____ , ____ , ____ , ____ , ____ , ____ ,

ROSE'S RESTAURANT

SANDWICHES

Tuna melt $1.50
Hamburger...........................$2.00
Cheeseburger $2.50
Double cheeseburger $3.00
Peanut butter/jelly $1.50
Egg salad $2.00
Hot dog................................$1.00
Chili dog $1.50

DRINKS

Cola, 7-Up, root beer..............$.50
Milk $1.00
Chocolate milk.......................$1.50
Lemonade $1.00
Iced tea $1.00
Milk shakes...........................$2.00
Coffee ....$.50
Juice ....$.50

SIDE DISHES

Potato salad $1.00
Cole slaw $1.00
Chips ....$.50
Fruit $1.50
Salad $1.50

DESSERTS

Ice cream $1.00
Apple pie $2.00
Frozen yogurt ....$.50
Hot fudge sundae $2.50
Cake $1.00

Developing Intelligences through Literature © 1996 Zephyr Press, Tucson, AZ

ROSE'S RESTAURANT

SANDWICHES

Tuna melt .... _____
Hamburger .... _____
Cheeseburger .... _____
Double cheeseburger .... _____
Peanut butter/jelly .... _____
Egg salad .... _____
Hot dog .... _____
Chili dog .... _____

DRINKS

Cola, 7-Up, root beer ..... _____
Milk .... _____
Chocolate milk .... _____
Lemonade .... _____
Iced tea .... _____
Milk shakes .... _____
Coffee .... _____
Juice .... _____

SIDE DISHES

Potato salad .... _____
Cole slaw .... _____
Chips .... _____
Fruit .... _____
Salad .... _____

DESSERTS

Ice cream .... _____
Apple pie .... _____
Frozen yogurt .... _____
Hot fudge sundae .... _____
Cake .... _____

ROSE'S CANDY STORE

Chocolate kisses ....5 pennies

Ribbon candy ....2 pennies

Tootsie Rolls...5 pennies

Butterscotch drops 1   penny

Taffy ....2 pennies

Lollipops...3 pennies

Candy bars .... 10 pennies

Fudge ....4 pennies

Rock candy ....5 pennies

Peanut brittle .... 10 pennies

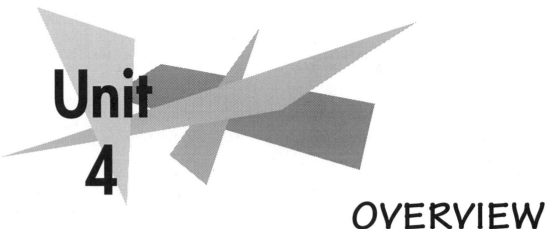

Unit 4

OVERVIEW

Central Literature Selection:
Over in the Meadow
by Laura Rose

Unit Focus: Reading Number Words
Grades: K–3

THINKING SKILLS SYMBOLS IDENTIFICATION				
Personal Connection	Creation	Mastery	Reasoning	Metacognition

MI ICON IDENTIFICATION						
Musical/ Rhythmic	Bodily/ Kinesthetic	Visual/ Spatial	Verbal/ Linguistic	Logical/ Mathematical	Interpersonal	Intrapersonal

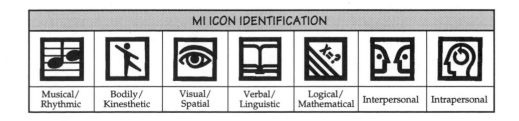

Lesson 1: **Free Reading with Literature Connections** (Grades K–3; twenty minutes a day)

Students read alone, in pairs, or in groups from a selection of books that are based on a number theme.

Lesson 2: **Favorite Read-Alouds** (Grades K–3; five to ten minutes a day)

Students keep track of read-alouds on the unit topic and vote for their favorite.

Lesson 3: **Adding Music** (Grades K–3; one class period)

Students learn to sing *Over in the Meadow* to a simple tune.

Lesson 4: **Which One?** (Grades K–3; one class period)

Students play a reasoning game by placing markers on number work sheets to answer math questions.

Lesson 5: **Singing Number Songs** (Grades K–3; one class period)

Students learn and sing number songs.

Lesson 6: **Personal Graphs** (Grades K–3; daily during unit)

Students respond individually to questions by answering with a number word and placing a personal marker on a classroom graph.

Lesson 7: **Writing Number Books** (Grades K–3; five to eight class periods)

After the class brainstorms some items they would love to have, each child writes a book in the number-book pattern to practice reading and writing number words in a creative format.

Lesson 8: **Calendar Big Book** (Grades K–3; two class periods)

Students create their own big book by entering their names and special school events in the spaces on a large calendar.

Lesson 9: **Write a Number Song** (Grades K–3; five to eight class periods)

Together the class composes and memorizes a holiday song in the number-book style. Students then copy each verse.

Lesson 10: **Read the Story on the Wall** (Grades 1–3; two class periods)

Working in groups, students illustrate pages of *Over in the Meadow* to create a bulletin board with text so the story can be read on the wall.

Synopsis of *Over in the Meadow*

Over in the Meadow is a delightful rhyming number book. In poetic style, each page describes a mother animal and her babies, who are having a wonderful time in their natural environment. With each page and each new mother, the number of babies grows by one until the final page on which the mother has ten little darlings. Since the text is so readable, students enjoy hearing it over and over, and even beginning first-graders are soon able to "read" many parts of it.

Explanation of Unit Focus: Reading Number Words

In the beginning grades, a meaningful focus centered around a reading skill can be very effective. Into the first few weeks of first, second, or third grade, this unit serves as a way to focus students' attention on the skill of reading number words while you introduce them to your style of teacher-made books and sustained silent reading. Each lesson is designed to help students develop the skill of reading number words and to understand how they are used. For kindergarten, the focus can be altered to reading numerals 1 though 10 and noticing them in literature.

Cross-Curricular Connections

You can find math and science activities where number words are used.

To Start the Unit

Look at the suggested lessons and select those that are appropriate for your class. Read *Over in the Meadow* aloud to your students, then proceed with any lesson you choose.

Literature Connections

Following is a list of books on the unit's focus for your students to read independently during the unit and even after you have finished the unit. If each student is reading a different book, discussions and activities regarding the unit's focus will be far richer than if everyone reads the same selection. See technique 1, Free Reading with Literature Connections, for suggestions.

Anno, Mitsumasa. 1983. *Anno's Mysterious Multiplying Jar.* Putnam.

Bang, Molly. 1983. *Ten, Nine, Eight.* Greenwillow.

Birch, David. 1988. *King's Chessboard.* Dial.

Carle, Eric. 1989. *1, 2, 3 to the Zoo.* Putnam.

Christelow, Eileen. 1989. *Five Little Monkeys Jumping on the Bed.* Clarion.

Clement, Rod. 1991. *Counting on Frank.* Gareth Stevens.

Crews, Donald. 1986. *Ten Black Dots.* Greenwillow.

DeRegniers, Beatrice Schenk. 1985. *So Many Cats.* Clarion.

Dunbar, Joyce. 1987. *A Cake for Barney.* Orchard.

Emberley, Barbara. 1992. *One Wide River to Cross.* Little, Brown.

Feelings, Tom. 1976. *Moja Means One: A Swahili Counting Book.* Dial.

Gerstein, Mordicai. 1988. *Roll Over!* Crown.

Giganti, Paul. 1988. *How Many Snails?* Greenwillow.

Hoban, Tana. 1987. *26 Letters and 99 Cents.* Greenwillow.

Hutchins, Pat. 1986. *The Doorbell Rang.* Greenwillow.

Keller, Holly. 1983. *Ten Sleepy Sheep.* Greenwillow.

Koontz, Robin Michael. 1988. *This Old Man: The Counting Song.* Dodd, Mead.

LeSeig, Theo. 1961. *Ten Apples Up on Top.* Random.

Lewin, Betsy. 1981. *Cat Count.* Dodd, Mead.

Linden, Ann Marie. 1992. *One Smiling Grandma.* Dial.

McLeod, Emilie. 1961. *One Snail and Me.* Little, Brown.

O'Donnell, Elizabeth. 1991. *Twelve Days of Summer.* Morrow.

Pallotta, Jerry. 1992. *Icky Bug Counting Book.* Charlesbridge.

Pittman, Helena Clare. 1986. *A Grain of Rice.* Hastings House.

Schwartz, David M. 1989. *If You Made a Million.* Lothrop, Lee & Shepard.

Scott, Ann Herbert. 1990. *One Good Horse.* Greenwillow.

Sendak, Maurice. 1962. *One Was Johnny.* Harper & Row.

Slobodkina, Esphyr. 1947. *Caps for Sale.* Harper.

Thornhill, Jan. 1989. *Wildlife 1-2-3: A Nature Counting Book.* Simon & Schuster.

Walsh, Ellen Stoll. 1991. *Mouse Count.* Harcourt Brace Jovanovich.

Warren, Cathy. 1983. *Ten-Alarm Camp-Out.* Lothrop, Lee & Shepard.

Lesson 1

FREE READING WITH LITERATURE CONNECTIONS

Materials

a large assortment of number books

Preparation

Go to a library and check out a variety of picture books that are based on numbers. It is great to get at least one for every other student (see Literature Connections, page 84, for suggestions).

Procedure

Have students read freely in self-directed books for an extended period (15–20 minutes) each day. This unit fits particularly well during the first week of the school year to introduce sustained silent reading. Most first-graders will not be able to read at the beginning of the year, and second- and third-graders need a comfortable review of material. Students will also report on their reading in some way (see technique 1, Free Reading with Literature Connections, page 267).

Multiple Intelligence Connections

Lesson 2

FAVORITE READ-ALOUDS

Materials

read-aloud books from literature connections or other books based on number words

Preparation

Photocopy the cover or title page, whichever has a more interesting picture, of each day's read-aloud selection.

Procedure

Read aloud to your class at least one story a day from your unit-oriented collection. After about a week, have students vote on their favorite. See technique 2, Read-Alouds, on page 268 for details.

Multiple Intelligence Connections

Lesson 3

ADDING MUSIC

Materials

any version of *Over in the Meadow*

Preparation

Practice singing *Over in the Meadow* to the tune of "Twinkle, twinkle, little star" or the 1920s tune "Boop, boop, dittum-dottum, wattum, choo" leaving in the nonsense chorus.

Procedure

Teach students how to sing *Over in the Meadow* to one of the tunes listed above or another tune that works. You may want to print the words of the story on a large song chart (see technique 3, Music Connections, page 270, for suggestions).

Multiple Intelligence Connections

 WHICH ONE?

Materials

a copy of work sheet 4-1, Which One? for each student

a marker (a button, a paper clip) for each student

Preparation

Photocopy work sheet 4-1 so you have enough for each student.

Procedure

Step 1: Distribute work sheet 4-1 to all students. Tell them that they are going to guess which word you are describing.

Step 2: First say each word in the order that it occurs on the work sheet, and have students place their marker on each as you say it. This activity gets them used to the rules of the game and ensures that all students are familiar with the words.

Step 3: Ask a question that will stimulate some thinking and have students place their markers by the word that they think is the right answer. There can be more than one correct answer for some of the questions, and that is just fine. Following are some examples of questions:

Which one tells how many fingers you have?

Which one tells how old you are?

Which one rhymes with fun?

Which one has a silent "e"?

Which one would be last in alphabetical order?

Which one is the number of windows in our classroom?

Step 4: After each question, ask students what they marked and why, and let them know that several answers may be correct. The discussion develops their thinking skills.

Step 5: After you have asked a few questions, invite students to think up some questions. Ask one child to question the class and have the rest place their markers on the work sheets. Then discuss the answers and the reasons behind them. Continue to call for other volunteers to question the class.

Step 6: You can repeat this game throughout the year, using words, pictures, or both, linking it with math, science, or literature. It is meant primarily to develop thinking, but it will also teach facts and skills such as learning to read the number words on this work sheet. Other subjects for a work sheet for this game could be

characters from a story

animals from a science unit

kinds of plants

color words

words from a poem with which the students are familiar

Additional Steps for Kindergarten

- Distribute work sheets with numerals instead of number words. In a multiage class, the kindergarten students can do their numeral work sheet while the older students do their word-oriented work sheets.

Multiple Intelligence Connections

Lesson 5

SINGING NUMBER SONGS

Materials

chart paper or materials to create a class big book

felt-tip markers

long pointer

good, singable number songs

Preparation

Gather some singable number songs such as "The Ants Go Marching One by One" or "Ten Little Angels in the Band." Read through technique 3, Music Connections, page 270, to learn how to make a song chart.

Procedure

Using the charts or big books you have prepared, teach students to read the words to the songs and to sing them.

Multiple Intelligence Connections

PERSONAL GRAPHS

Materials

a large pocket chart with number words from one to ten across the bottom axis

individual photos of all your students

Preparation

See technique 4, Making Pocket Charts, on page 271 for instructions to make the graph; mount it where students can see it easily. Write out the question of the day, a question that can be answered by a number word from one to ten, and post it next to the empty graph.

Procedure

Step 1: Pick a time of day when students can approach the graph and place their photos or markers on the numbers of their choice. You might choose one or more of the following times:

As students enter the room before the school day begins

As they finish washing up for lunch

As they complete another assignment

As part of the getting-ready-to-go-home activities

As part of one of your rotating math or reading stations

Step 2: Students approach the graph in small groups and try to read the question of the day. They can help each other by giving hints and phonics clues only; they should not read it for each other. If you model this kind of help a few times, students will pick up your strategies and help each other. Following are some number-related questions that you might use:

How old are you?

Which grade are you in? (for multiage classrooms)

How many people live where you live?

How many pets do you own?

How many teeth have you lost?

How many brothers and sisters do you have?

How many TV shows did you watch last night?

How old will you be on your next birthday?

What is your favorite number from one to ten?

Step 3: After students decipher the question of the day, they place their photos or markers in the columns that properly answer the question for them.

Step 4: At some time in the school day, draw the students' attention to the completed graph and discuss the data. Compare and contrast by asking questions such as the following:

Which number has the most students' markers?

Which number has more than three markers?

Which number has less than one marker?

Which two numbers have the same number of markers?

Which number has two less than another number?

Step 5: Once students have learned how to use this graph, you can continue to use it daily throughout the year. It effectively provides each student one brief, meaningful opportunity each day to decode unfamiliar print.

Additional Steps for Kindergarten

- Read the question to the students. If you have a kindergarten-only class, use numbers rather than number words on the graph. If you have a multiage class, let the older students in the small groups help kindergartners translate the number words into numbers.

Multiple Intelligence Connections

WRITING NUMBER BOOKS

Materials for the Teacher

felt-tip pens

three large sheets of chart paper for brainstorming

Materials for Each Student

pencils, crayons, or felt-tip pens

a teacher-made book

a copy of parent note 4-1

Preparation

To make books for students, alternate 5 sheets of lined paper and 6 sheets of drawing paper. (See technique 5, Teacher-Made Books, on page 273 for a description.) Mount on the wall 3 sheets of chart paper next to each other. Copy parent note 4-1 for each student.

Procedure

Step 1: Read *Over in the Meadow* and several other books with a similar pattern in which each page has one more number than the previous page.

Step 2: Tell students they will create their own number books like those you have been reading.

Step 3: Write the number word *one* at the top of the first sheet of chart paper. Ask students what they might like to own one of—a castle, a parrot, or what? As they give suggestions, record five to ten words on the third chart, across from the number one (see example below).

Step 4: Return to the second chart and ask what color each of the items they have named might be. Record those colors on the second chart next to the item they match (see example below).

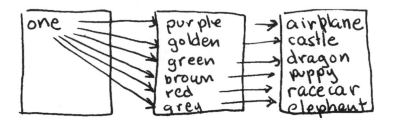

Step 5: Give students a teacher-made book and tell them to turn to the first page. Ask them to choose their favorite ideas from the charts to write in their own books. Beginning writers could write repeating sentences, such as "I'd like *one* purple airplane." More experienced writers could compose their own sentences to include the three words, such as "I would love to fly in *one* purple airplane."

Step 6: As each student completes the printing, check for correctness and then authorize the student to begin drawing an appropriate illustration on the facing page.

Step 7: On subsequent days, repeat this process, adding one or two number pages daily. As you add more pages to brainstorming charts, save the old ones to help absent students catch up.

Step 8: When books are completed, students can select and mark their best pages (metacognition). Photocopy these pages and place them in your student's portfolios.

Step 9: Students read their books to themselves and to about five others, and sign the backs of partners' books. Send books home for homework with the parent note.

Additional Steps for Kindergarten

- Students write only the number on each book page and draw the matching number of items.

Multiple Intelligence Connections

CALENDAR BIG BOOK

Materials

a current yearly calendar with lovely pictures and large daily spaces to write in

optional: photocopied photographs of the faces of all your class members

Preparation

Obtain a good calendar, a list of school holidays and events, and a list of your class members' birthdays. Print each holiday and event along with its month and day on a separate scrap of paper for students to copy from.

Procedure

Step 1: Show students the calendar you have found. Look through it, discussing the pictures and the months.

Step 2: Tell students that together you will be transforming this calendar into a big book to add to your class library.

Step 3: Show students how to record their birthdays on the calendar squares by first recording your own birthday:

```
┌──────────────────────────┐
│ 21                       │
│                          │
│   Today is Mrs. Rose's   │
│     birthday!            │
│                          │
└──────────────────────────┘
```

If more than one child shares a birthday, both must write their names on the same square. If you have photocopies of students' photographs, students can glue their own pictures onto the calendar squares above their sentences.

Step 4: Arrange for all students to take a turn to write their birthdays into the calendar. You might extend this activity throughout the school day as you go on to teach other subjects, or you might do it during reading station time.

Step 5: The next day, ask students to help you fill in all of the holidays and school vacations and special events. Show them your list of these days, and as you name each event, ask for a volunteer to enter that special day in the calendar. Give each volunteer the paper on which you recorded the words to describe the special event so he or she can copy them (see example below).

Christmas Day

Step 6: Again, let students record their entries, along with pictures if appropriate, during the rest of the day. When complete, read the calendar aloud to the class and add it to your class library. Students will enjoy reading it to themselves and to each other all year long.

Additional Steps for Kindergarten

- Students can shorten their birthday entries to just their name or to "Caitlin's birthday." You can make the other special day entries with students watching and giving you ideas for the drawings.

Multiple Intelligence Connections

WRITE A NUMBER SONG

Materials for the Teacher

chart paper

chorus of song on page 104

felt-tip pens

Materials for the Students

teacher-made books

pencils, crayons, or felt-tip pens

optional: star stamp

Preparation

Read or reread *Over in the Meadow.* If you have a recording of the song, play the recording. Create teacher-made books with six half-sheets of drawing paper and five half-sheets of lined paper according to the directions in technique 5, Teacher-Made Books, on page 273. Cut ten stars from cardboard and cover them with gold or silver glitter. Learn the melody of the "Star Song" on page 104.

Note: I first created this song and lesson because I needed a secular song for our school-wide Christmas season program. Closer to a different holiday, this song could as easily be revised to ten pumpkins shining in the night, ten bunnies hopping through the grass, or ten hearts shining on Valentine's Day.

Procedure

Step 1: Write the word *one* at the top of the chart paper. Tell students that they will be writing a song, and ask them to help you list rhyming words on your chart below the word *one* (see example below; also see page 103 for a list of rhymes for each of the number words through 10.)

one

fun   sun   begun   run   bun   none   spun   done

Step 2: Sing the first line of the "Star Song": "Shine little stars as we hang one." Hum the next line so that students can sense the rhythm. Ask for their suggestions, and write them on the chart paper. Help your students with hints as they try to fit their ideas into the cadence of the song. For instance, students might suggest the following:

We'll hang stars until we're done.

Hanging stars is lots of fun.

Christmas stars shine like the sun.

We have only just begun.

Step 3: After you record their ideas, let students vote for their favorites. Then write in the class favorite at the top of a fresh sheet of chart paper where all the verses for the song will eventually be recorded, or write the lines on sentence strips for a pocket chart.

> *Shine little stars as we hang one,*
> *Hanging one is lots of fun.*

Step 4: Now ask students to copy those two lines into their own books and either draw one star or use a star stamp to illustrate the one star page.

Step 5: The next day, begin by singing as much of the song as is written and include the chorus (page 104). Then repeat the process in step 4 for the next number. Continue each day until all of the numbers are done and the song is finished. Now students can sing the song either as you point to the words on the song chart or from the books that they have written. For a performance, ask ten volunteer soloists to sing one verse each. Ask the first volunteer to sing the first verse and hang one star on the painted tree while the class sings the chorus. After the class sings the chorus, follow with the second volunteer and continue the routine until the song is completed. To give you an idea of what can be done, following are the verses that my first-grade class wrote:

> *Shine little stars as we hang one,*
> *hanging one is lots of fun.*
>
> *Shine little stars as we hang two,*
> *Christmas is fun for me and you.*
>
> *Shine little stars as we hang three,*
> *put up the stockings and light the tree.*
>
> *Shine little stars as we hang four,*
> *milk for Santa I will pour.*
>
> *Shine little stars as we hang five,*
> *Rudolph through the sky will dive.*
>
> *Shine little stars as we hang six,*
> *get out the candles and light the wicks.*
>
> *Shine little stars as we hang seven,*
> *stars are shining up in heaven.*
>
> *Shine little stars as we hang eight,*
> *Christmas is coming, we can hardly wait.*
>
> *Shine little stars as we hang nine,*
> *oh, how the Christmas lights do shine.*
>
> *Shine little stars as we hang ten,*
> *it's such a good song, let's sing it again.*

My students thought of five or six possibilities for each line, and they didn't always choose the one I liked best. I preferred "peace on earth, good will toward men" for the last line, but I was overwhelmingly outvoted in favor of "it's such a good song, let's sing it again." It was, and they did.

Multiple Intelligence Connections

READ THE STORY ON THE WALL

Materials

a blank bulletin board

one copy of each page of the text of *Over in the Meadow*

assorted colored paper

scissors

pencils

a stapler

Preparation

Read or reread *Over in the Meadow.*

Procedure

Step 1: Reread *Over in the Meadow* and invite students to chime in whenever they can.

Step 2: Show students the blank bulletin board and tell them that they will be drawing their own pictures about this story so that they will soon all be able to read the wall.

Step 3: Divide the class into eleven groups. Assign each group a number from one to eleven. (If you have more than twenty-two students, put the extra children into the groups that deal with the higher numbers, as they will have more drawing to do.)

Step 4: Ask each group to illustrate a different page from *Over in the Meadow*. Tell them to draw and cut out the element of each setting (such as a stream, a tree with a hole in it, or reeds and a shore) from construction paper. Also ask them to draw and cut out the mother and correct number of babies for their assigned page. Group 11 will be responsible for putting the title and author on the bulletin board and for decorating the borders and putting up background paper. They will also staple or pin the ten pages of text across the bulletin board in some kind of reasonable order so that the rest of the groups will know where to locate their illustrations.

Step 5: With your help, students will work on their illustrations. If you have an adult helper available, ask that person to help group 11 with the bulletin board. When each group's illustration is drawn and cut out, check the results. Then instruct that group to go to the bulletin board, locate their page by reading the text that is up on the board, and arrange and staple their illustration to the board near the paper that displays their text.

Step 6: Since groups will finish at various times, provide a low-supervision activity as each group finishes, such as reading one of the number books you have gathered for this unit.

Step 7: When the board is completed (it might take more than one period), ask the class to look at the bulletin board and read the story aloud with you. As they help you analyze the order in which the pages should be read, pin a length of yarn connecting each page to the next. After reading each page, students can applaud for the illustrators.

Step 8: Read this story together with the class each day for the next week or so, and encourage students in their free time to use a pointer and read the wall.

More Challenge

Instead of providing a copy of the story's text, let each group be responsible for copying it neatly to post with their illustrations.

Unit
4

MATERIALS

Five	One
Four	Six
Three	Two

Work Sheet 4-1: Which One?
Kindergarten

5	1
4	6
3	2

Dear Parent,

As part of our study of children's literature, your child has written and illustrated this book. He or she should be able to read it to you, and I hope you will take the time to listen to it and discuss the words and the pictures. After your child reads this book to you, perhaps you can add it to your home library of children's books. In the future, you might sometimes choose to read this book along with those by more famous authors.

I hope you enjoy and express your pride in your child's work.

Sincerely,

List of Rhyming Words

When you write your version with your students, you may find the following rhyming words helpful. (Let students try to think of them first, but give hints as needed.)

One: *done, fun, none, spun, stun, run, undone, son, spun*

Two: *shoe, who, you, ado, canoe, outdo, shampoo, too, to, through, taboo, goo*

Three: *see, me, bee, knee, she, tea, decree, degree, jubilee, sea, free, glee, he, spree, oversee*

Four: *door, more, galore, store, before, war, pour, tore, wore, days of yore, implore, evermore, sycamore, score, soar*

Five: *arrive, alive, drive, dive, deprive, survive*

Six: *fix, mix, sticks, politics, licks, picks, nix, tricks, bricks, wicks, kicks,*

Seven: *heaven, Kevin, Devon, leaven*

Eight: *gate, late, straight, fate, great, grate, plate, create, celebrate, wait*

Nine: *fine, dine, mine, shine, line, pine, sign, twine, design, divine*

Ten: *men, then, again, hen, wren, pen, Ben, when*

Shine lit-tle stars as we hang one.   Hang-ing one is lots of fun.

Chorus:

Shine   star,   shine for me,   Shine like hope on a Christ-mas tree.

Unit 5

OVERVIEW

Central Literature Selections:

The Bears on Hemlock Mountain
by Alice Dagliesh
Keep the Lights Burning, Abbie
by Peter and Connie Roop

Unit Focus: Courage
Grades: 1–3

THINKING SKILLS SYMBOLS IDENTIFICATION				
Personal Connection	Creation	Mastery	Reasoning	Metacognition

MI ICON IDENTIFICATION						
Musical/ Rhythmic	Bodily/ Kinesthetic	Visual/ Spatial	Verbal/ Linguistic	Logical/ Mathematical	Interpersonal	Intrapersonal

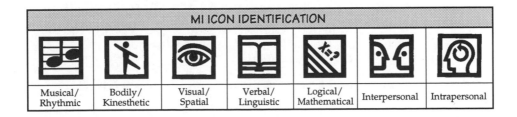

Lesson 1: **Response Journals** (Grades 2–3; five minutes or more each day)

As the chapters are read, students make thoughtful responses in a teacher-made book.

Lesson 2: **Free Reading with Literature Connections** (Grades 1–3; twenty minutes a day)

Students spend time each day reading and sharing books related to the unit focus.

Lesson 3: **Favorite Read-Alouds** (Grades 1–3; five to ten minutes each day)

Students keep track of all read-alouds connected to the unit focus and vote for their favorites.

Lesson 4: **I Am Proud** (Grades 1–3; one or two class periods)

Students talk and write about something that they did alone for the first time.

Lesson 5: **Sing a Chant** (Grades 1–3; fifteen minutes)

Students learn and add a tune to the chant in chapter 5 of *The Bears on Hemlock Mountain*.

Lesson 6: **Acts of Courage** (Grades 1–3; one or two class periods)

Students ask parents for help in remembering a time when they were courageous. These incidents are compiled into a class book on courage.

Lesson 7: **Instant Research** (Grades 1–3; one class period)

This motivational research strategy teaches students how we learn through reading informational material.

Lesson 8: **Building Lighthouses** (Grades 1–3; two or three class periods)

Students create lighthouses from the models provided in Lesson 6 and may write descriptions of their creations.

Lesson 9: **Venn Diagrams** (Grades 1–3; one class period)

Students compare and contrast Jonathan from *The Bears on Hemlock Mountain* with Abbie from *Keep the Lights Burning, Abbie*.

Lesson 10: **Plan and Perform** (Grades 1–3; four to five afternoon class periods)

Students plan and do a performance of one of the literature selections.

Lesson 11: **Courage Is** (Grades 1–3; one or two class periods)

Students brainstorm and write a class book about courage.

Synopsis of *The Bears on Hemlock Mountain*

In this story a boy must go over a mountain to get a cooking pot for a celebration. Rumors of bears on Hemlock Mountain haunt him as he goes over and back. Because of a late start, he finds himself on the mountain as dark is falling, and the bears do appear. The tale explores how Jonathan finds courage in a frightening situation.

Synopsis of *Keep the Lights Burning, Abbie*

This true story describes the efforts of Abbie Burgess, a little girl who kept the lighthouse lights shining though a month-long storm while her father was away and her mother lay ill.

Explanation of Unit Focus: Courage

Students explore their inner selves as they think about courage, their own and that of other children in literature and real life. This unit helps students define an abstract idea for themselves.

Cross-Curricular Connections

An effective connection can be made with study of community helpers who show courage in keeping the community safe. The unit also ties in with any units on self-protection, dealing with strangers, and with emergencies.

To Start the Unit

Look at the suggested lessons and select those that are appropriate for your class. Proceed with any lesson you choose.

Literature Connections

Following is a list of books on the unit's focus for your students to read independently during the unit and even after you have finished the unit. If each student is reading a different book, discussions and activities regarding the unit's focus will be far richer than if everyone reads the same selection. See technique 1, Free Reading with Literature Connections, for suggestions.

Picture Books

Alexander, Martha. 1989. *Move Over, Twerp*. Dial.

Brenner, Barbara. 1984. *Wagon Wheels*. Harper.

Bunting, Eve. 1984. *Ghost's Hour, Spook's Hour*. Clarion.

Carrick, Carol. 1984. *Dark and Full of Secrets*. Clarion.

Chaffin, Lillie D. 1980. *We Be Warm Till Springtime Comes*. Macmillan.

Cohen, Miriam. 1981. *Jim Meets the Thing*. Greenwillow.

Crowe, Robert. 1976. *Clyde Monster*. Dutton.

Gackenbach, Dick. 1984. *Harry and the Terrible Whatzit*. Clarion.

Hilleary, Jane K. 1968. *Fletcher and the Great Big Dog*. Houghton Mifflin.

Hort, Lenny. 1987. *The Boy Who Held Back the Sea*. Dial.

Jeffers, Susan. 1976. *Wild Robin*. Dutton.

Joose, Barbara. 1983. *Spiders in the Cellar*. Knopf.

Kellogg, Steven. 1973. *Island of the Skog*. Dial.

LeGuin, Ursula. 1992. *A Ride on the Red Mare's Back*. Orchard.

Lionni, Leo. 1960. *Inch by Inch*. Astor.

Martin, Bill. 1985. *Ghost-Eye Tree*. Holt.

McKissack, Patricia. 1986. *Flossie and the Fox*. Dial.

Meyer, Mercer. 1976. *Liza Lou and the Yeller Belly Swamp*. Four Winds.

————. 1993. *There's a Nightmare in My Closet*. Dial.

Mitchell, Margaree. 1993. *Uncle Ned's Barbershop*. Simon & Schuster.

Olson, Arielle. 1987. *Lighthouse Keeper's Daughter*. Little.

Peet, Bill. 1979. *Cowardly Clyde*. Houghton Mifflin.

Pittman, Helena Clare. 1988. *Once When I Was Scared*. Dutton.

Polacco, Patricia. 1990. *Thunder Cake*. Putnam.

Reeves, Mona. 1989. *The Spooky, Eerie Night Noise*. Bradbury.

Sendak, Maurice. 1981. *Outside Over There*. Harper.

Steig, William. 1986. *Brave Irene*. Farrar, Straus and Giroux.

Van Woerkem, Dorothy. 1978. *Alexandra the Rockeater*. Knopf.

Williams, Jay. 1976. *Everyone Knows What a Dragon Looks Like*. Four Winds.

Winthrop, Elizabeth. 1987. *Maggie and the Monster*. Holiday.

Longer Books

Aiken, Joan. 1987. *Moon's Revenge.* Knopf.
Crofford, Emily. 1981. *Matter of Pride.* Carolrhoda.
Dagliesh, Alice. 1987. *Courage of Sarah Noble.* Macmillan.
Fife, Dale. 1978. *North of Danger.* Dutton.
Fleischman, Paul. 1980. *Half-a-Moon Inn.* Harper.
Gardam, Jane. 1981. *Bridget and William.* Watts.
Houston, James. 1981. *Long Claws.* Atheneum.
McSwigan, Marie. 1942. *Snow Treasure.* Dutton.
Slote, Alfred. 1973. *Hang Tough, Paul Mather.* Lippencott.
Sperry, Armstrong. 1971. *Call It Courage.* Macillan.

Lesson 1

RESPONSE JOURNALS

Materials

teacher-made books

pencils

Preparation

For each student, make a book with 6 white pages and 5 lined pages (see technique 5, Teacher-Made Books, on page 273). If you are unused to response journals, be sure to refer to technique 10, Response Journals, page 281 for an overview of how to ensure the most student involvement.

Designed to stimulate students' thoughtful interaction with the story, this lesson will take about a week during the reading of *The Bears on Hemlock Mountain*. I have included specific exercises to do in the response journals after each chapter, but if other, better questions or work occur to you, do not hesitate to substitute them for mine. Always be aware, however, of a student's need for privacy, of being able to choose whether or not to share life events with you.

Procedure

Step 1: After reading chapter 1, have students list activities they have done all alone for the first time, share their lists with partners, and then underline those that both partners have written. (The underlining is done to keep the students focused on their conversation.)

Step 2: Ask students to raise hands and share their lists with you so that you can make a class list.

Optional Step 3: Do lesson 4, I Am Proud (have students choose one event to describe and illustrate).

Step 4: After reading chapter 2, talk about animals that your students would like to see in real life. Then ask students to draw and write about their personal choices and to give reasons for their choices. Talk about whether those choices might be dangerous. You might make a class graph of most-often chosen animals children want to see in real life.

Step 5: After reading chapters 3 and 4, have students draw and write whether or not they think that Jonathan will find bears on Hemlock Mountain, and what he might do. Their responses could be as simple as "Yes, he will meet bears," or "No, he won't."

Step 6: After reading chapter 5, do lesson 5.

Step 7: While reading chapter 8, have students chant along with you. Add a beat with a musical instrument. At the end of the chapter take a vote to show who thinks the dark shapes are really bears and who doesn't. Students could turn to partners to discuss what else the shapes might be.

Step 8: After reading chapters 9 and 10, have students record what helped Jonathan be brave. They will help you make a list of what helps them be brave when they are frightened. You can add what helps you as well.

Multiple Intelligence Connections

FREE READING WITH LITERATURE CONNECTIONS

Materials

books from the literature connections list or any other books about children who bravely face a difficult situation

Preparation

Gather a variety of books of different lengths and reading levels (see Literature Connections, page 108, for suggestions).

Procedure

Have students select and read a book from your unit collection for an extended period each day and also have them engage in some form of reporting on their reading to the class. See technique 1, Free Reading with Literature Connections, page 267, for more information.

Multiple Intelligence Connections

FAVORITE READ-ALOUDS

Lesson 3

Materials

fairly short read-aloud selections that are on the unit's topic of childhood courage

Preparation

Photocopy the cover or title page, whichever has a more interesting picture, of each day's read-aloud selection.

Procedure

Read aloud to your class at least one story a day from your unit-oriented collection. After about a week, let students vote on their favorite. See technique 2, Read-Alouds, on page 268 for details.

Multiple Intelligence Connections

Lesson 4

I AM PROUD

Materials

story paper

pencils, felt-tip pens, or crayons

Preparation

Read chapter 1 of *The Bears on Hemlock Mountain* and do the first activity in lesson 1, Response Journals, or have students brainstorm a list of things they have done all alone for the first time.

Procedure

Step 1: Review the list you brainstormed in preparation for the lesson.

Step 2: Give students story paper and ask them to select and write about one event of which they are most proud. Have them illustrate it (see example below).

When I stayed at Grandma's house I went to the store all by myself.

Step 3: As students work, circulate and check spelling and punctuation. When students finish their printing, help them correct any errors and perhaps write a little more detail.

Step 4: When the papers are completed and illustrated, collect them to create a class book. Read the book aloud to the students and add it to your class library.

Optional Step 5: Before collecting the papers, have students pair up and read to each other. Students can sign the backs of one another's papers and then go on to read to another partner until everyone has shared at least six times.

Additional Step for First Grade

- Students can work from a frame sentence that you have written on the board, such as "I am proud of the first time I _____ _____ all by myself." Those who are capable of writing more can be encouraged to do so.

Multiple Intelligence Connections

Lesson 5

SING A CHANT

Materials

The Bears on Hemlock Mountain

chart paper

felt-tip pens

Preparation

Print the words to the chant from chapter 5 on chart paper. Read the chapter aloud.

Procedure

Step 1: have students learn the chant in chapter 5 and repeat it with you. Have a volunteer point to the words as the class says them.

Step 2: With the class's help, make up a tune to go with the chant; add a drum beat and perhaps some other instruments.

Multiple Intelligence Connections

Lesson 6

ACTS OF COURAGE

Materials for Each Student

a copy of parent note 5-1
story paper
pencils

Preparation

Make a copy of the parent note 5-1 for each student.

Procedure

Step 1: Read through chapter 7 or 8 of *The Bears on Hemlock Mountain.*

Step 2: Tell students that each of them has done brave things, too. Share a story of something courageous that you did as a child. It could be as simple as going to sleep even though you thought there was a monster under your bed.

Step 3: Give each student a copy of parent note 5-1, the homework note. Read it with them and explain that they will be trying to remember a time when they were courageous.

Step 4: The next day, have students read or tell about their homework to a series of partners. Then ask students to illustrate their stories.

Step 5: Bind all the courageous stories into a class book and read it aloud. Because the printing was done at home and may be incorrect, you might want to make needed corrections and type them all or go through an editing process with the students.

More Challenge

Students learn the format of a newspaper report; who, what, when, where, and why are told in the first paragraph. Read some newspaper articles aloud and let students answer the five questions as you read. Then ask them to write their own stories of courage in newspaper format. You could then publish a class newspaper with all of the class's courageous acts in it.

Multiple Intelligence Connections

Lesson 7

INSTANT RESEARCH

Materials for Each Student

a copy of work sheet 5-1, Lighthouses

crayons or felt-tip pens

pencils

Materials for the Teacher

a copy of the fact sheet 5-1, Lighthouses

Preparation

Duplicate work sheet 5-1 for each student. Read or reread *Keep the Lights Burning, Abbie.*

Procedure for Grades 1 and 2

The following technique is highly effective and motivating because it is designed to get students to listen carefully when new information is presented. Because they are looking at pictures of the subject of the conversation, they should be more focused. After they have shared what they know and what they don't know, they are much more interested in hearing more about the subject.

Step 1: Give each student a copy of work sheet 5-1. Ask students to tell you what they know about lighthouses. Discuss their ideas for a few minutes. When uncertainties arise, let students know that you will be reading more information about the subject in just a minute.

Step 2: Read fact sheet 5-1 aloud to your class. Then ask students to turn their papers over and write at least three things that they just learned about lighthouses. So that all students can write at the same time, you might like to let them use their best-guess spelling.

Step 3: As students finish (some may be able to write only one or two facts, but encourage them to write more if possible), have them raise their hands and quietly read to you what they have written. Then have them turn their papers over and color the lighthouses until everyone has finished writing the facts.

Step 4: Collect and read at least some of the students' writing aloud to the class.

Procedure for Grade 3

Step 1: Proceed as you would for the earlier grades, but ask students to record at least five new facts.

Step 2: To help them record the facts, read the fact sheet again after most students have written at least two facts. This time ask students to raise their hands whenever you mention a fact that they have written down. With this second reading, most students will be able to remember at least five facts.

Step 3: Continue as with the earlier grades.

Note: Have your students keep work sheet 5-1 for use in the next lesson.

Multiple Intelligence Connections

BUILDING LIGHTHOUSES

Materials

work sheet 5-1, Lighthouses

paper plates

empty paper towel rolls

construction paper

felt-tip markers

glue

scissors

Preparation

Read or reread *Keep the Lights Burning, Abbie*. Gather empty paper towel rolls and the other construction materials. Photocopy work sheet 5-1 for each student if you have not already done so for lesson 6, Instant Research.

Procedure

Optional Step 1: Do lesson 6, Instant Research.

Step 2: Discuss the different lighthouses pictured on work sheet 5-1 and why they were designed as shown.

Step 3: Using the paper plates as the island base on which the lighthouse will be built, let students work independently or with partners to design and build their lighthouses out of the paper towel cores and whatever other materials they can think of.

Step 4: Show students how to make a cone of construction paper for the tower's roof (see figure 5-1).

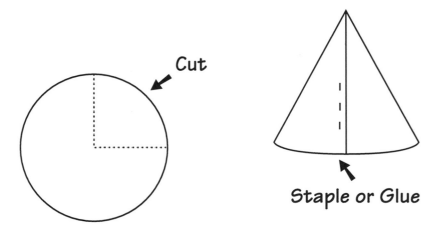

Figure 5-1. Making a cone from construction paper

More Challenge (for grade 3 or a small group of grade 2)

Have students write individual descriptions of their lighthouses that are so detailed that someone else could find the lighthouse described. As students are working on their descriptions, give them plenty of assistance, and let them know if they need more detail in their descriptions. Then do one of the following:

- Arrange all of the lighthouses in one part of the room. Read each description and ask a volunteer student to point it out. Have the class agree or disagree by vote. As each lighthouse that matches a description is found, it is given back to its owner.

- Be sure that each student's name is written under his or her lighthouse. Place the lighthouses randomly on the students' desks. Give each student a description with the name of its author attached. Challenge everyone to read the description he or she has been given, find the matching lighthouse, and sit down in that seat. At a signal from you, everyone looks for a name under the lighthouse. If it matches their description they remain seated; if it does not, they get up and start their search again. Repeat until all are correctly matched.

Optional Step 5: Students share with each other what was helpful in the directions and make suggestions for improvements.

Multiple Intelligence Connections

Lesson 9

VENN DIAGRAMS

Materials

a copy of *Keep the Lights Burning, Abbie* or another book about a courageous child

an overhead transparency of work sheet 5-2, Venn Diagram

markers

Preparation

Make an overhead transparency of work sheet 5-2 or copy it onto a chart. Both stories, *The Bears on Hemlock Mountain* and *Keep the Lights Burning, Abbie,* should have been read or reread so as to be fresh in the students' minds.

Procedure

Step 1: Show the Venn diagram; label one circle Abbie and the other Jonathan.

Step 2: Ask students to write down at least one detail that describes Jonathan only, one that describes Abbie only, and one that describes both.

Optional Step 3: Have students pair up and add their partners' ideas to their lists, and also add any more that they both think of.

Step 4: Ask students to share what they have written and add even more character traits to help you fill in your large Venn diagram (see example below).

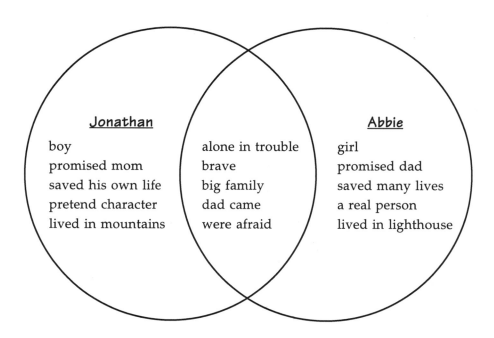

More Challenge

Students make their own Venn diagrams comparing themselves with either Jonathan or Abbie.

Multiple Intelligence Connections

Lesson 10

PLAN AND PERFORM

Materials

for each group, a copy of one of the two central literature selections
props for students' performances

Preparation

Read technique 8, Book Groups, page 278. At least once before this lesson, read both central literature selections aloud to the class.

Procedure

Step 1: Ask students to select one of the two books to act out. Assign students to heterogeneous groups of four to six according to their preference.

Step 2: Help the class brainstorm a list of ways to act out their stories as one or more members of their groups read aloud the book to the class. You will find some good suggestions in technique 8.

Step 3: Give students several work periods to plan and practice a creative way of acting out the story using work sheet 5-3, Intentions and Reflections (page 129), to help them monitor their progress. Read technique 7, Intentions and Reflections, for more information.

Step 4: Have the groups perform for one another.

Step 5: After each performance, ask the rest of the class to write a compliment to the group. While the audience is writing, have the performers write something about their individual performances about which they are proud.

Multiple Intelligence Connections

Lesson 11

COURAGE IS

Materials for Each Student

story paper

pencils

crayons or felt-tip pens

Materials for the Teacher

a chart

markers

Preparation

By this time, your students should have read both the central literature selections.

Procedure

Step 1: Write "Courage is" at the top of the chart paper or chalkboard.

Step 2: Ask all students to tell you what courage is, and list their responses on the chart or chalkboard (see example).

Courage is . . .

Sleeping without a night-light

Being home alone

Walking through the woods alone

Standing up to a bully

Defending your friend when people insult him or her

Not letting anyone push you around

Not taking drugs

Admitting that you did something wrong and taking your punishment

---

Step 3: As you make the list, take time to discuss the idea of courage, and let students know that you have courage when you are afraid to do something but do it anyway. Emphasize the little acts of courage that happen every day.

Step 4: Give students story paper and have them select one of the ideas that were brainstormed by the class. Ask them to write about and illustrate the idea, starting with "Courage is . . ." (see example).

"Courage is standing up to a bully even if he is bigger than you."

Courage is _____

Step 5: When the papers are completed, bind them into a class book about courage and read it aloud to the class. Add it to your classroom library.

Unit
5

MATERIALS

Dear Parents,

We have been reading *The Bears on Hemlock Mountain* by Alice Dagliesh. It is the story of a boy who faces the possibility of running into bears while he is doing a favor for his mother. We would like you to help your child think of something that he or she has done that took courage. It might be as simple as going to sleep with the light off or going for a ride on a merry-go-round. Or it might be calling 911 in an emergency, or keeping a brother or sister from getting hurt.

After you and your child discuss courage for a while and decide which story to tell, would you please help him or her write it on the attached paper to read to our class at school tomorrow?

Thank you very much for your help.

Sincerely,

Work Sheet 5-1
Lighthouses

Fact Sheet 5-1

Lighthouses

People began building lighthouses more than two thousand years ago, when they first began sailing ships far out to sea. When night fell, sailors could not see the coast and they were in danger of running aground, sinking their ships, and drowning. Lighthouses have saved many lives because sailors saw the light and turned their ships away from the rocks and shore.

Lighthouses are never built inland, but always right on the most dangerous points of land and rock. Because of these locations, some of the first lighthouses were knocked down and swept away by ocean storms. Eventually, people learned how to build lighthouses that could remain standing through any storm.

Because they were built so far away from cities and towns, lighthouses were usually someone's home. Sometimes the home is next to the light's tower, but sometimes the people lived right in the lighthouse where each room was up above another. To go from the kitchen to the bedroom, you climbed the stairs. Then to get to the next room, you climbed the stairs again. Many lighthouses had a whole room just for their library, because reading books was the only entertainment people living in lighthouses had, other than watching the sea. Today, most lighthouses have automatically controlled lights and no longer need people to take care of them, so few have anyone living in them.

Lighthouses are built in many shapes. Many are round. This shape takes up the least amount of space because the houses are built on small rocks and jetties. Some are only short towers built on the tops of houses if the lighthouses are on such high cliffs that they don't need to be any taller. Short lighthouses have also been built on ships, but this proved to be dangerous, because in a dense fog, ships could not see the light and would run into the lighthouse boat.

As long as ships sail the sea, the lighthouse will be a welcome sight, warning the sailors that they are close to land.

Work Sheet 5-2
Venn Diagram

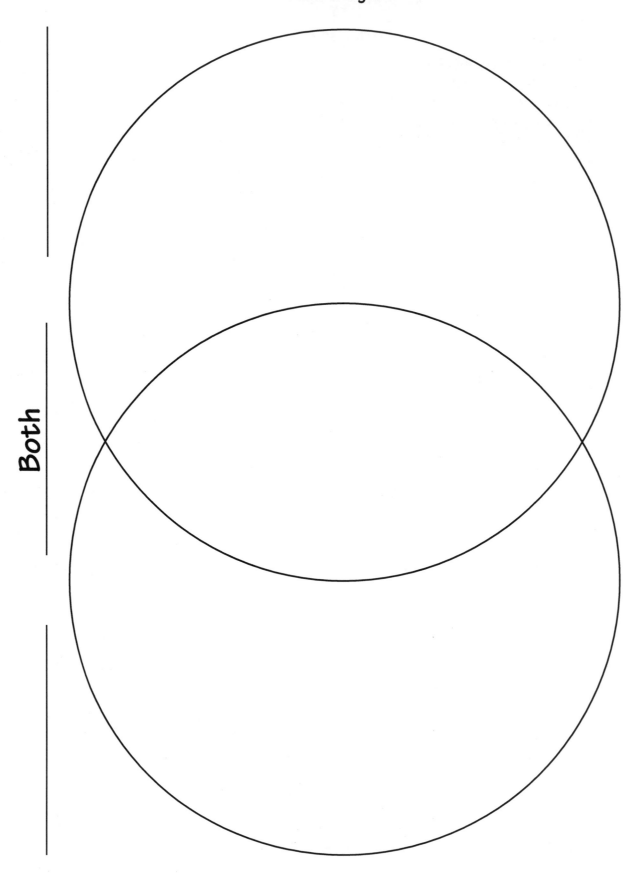

Both

Work Sheet 5-3
Intentions and Reflections
Adding Metacognition to Projects

Date: _____ Today I intend to _____

_____

_____

_____

During this work period, I was able to _____

_____

_____

Tomorrow I hope to

_____

_____

- -

Date: _____ Today I intend to _____

_____

_____

_____

During this work period, I was able to _____

_____

_____

Tomorrow I hope to

_____

_____

- -

Note: For longer projects use additional sheets or have students use a teacher-made journal to make similar daily entries.

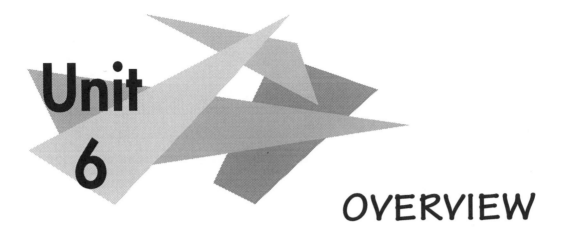

Unit 6

OVERVIEW

Central Literature Selection:
When I Was Young in the Mountains
by Cynthia Rylant

Unit Focus:
Needs of Children through Time and Space
Grades: 1–6

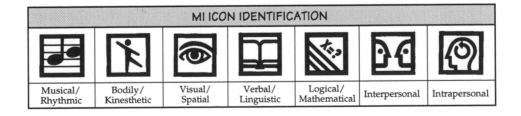

THINKING SKILLS SYMBOLS IDENTIFICATION				
Personal Connection	Creation	Mastery	Reasoning	Metacognition

MI ICON IDENTIFICATION						
Musical/ Rhythmic	Bodily/ Kinesthetic	Visual/ Spatial	Verbal/ Linguistic	Logical/ Mathematical	Interpersonal	Intrapersonal

Lesson 1: **Free Reading with Literature Connections** (Grades 1–3; every day during unit)

Students read various books that focus on the theme of common needs of children. Periodic brief reports and an optional book presentation are made to the class.

Lesson 2: **Favorite Read-Alouds** (Grades 1–3; five to ten minutes a day)

Each day, students spend time reading and sharing books related to the unit focus.

Lesson 3: **Common Needs** (Grades 1–6; one class period)

Students brainstorm a list of elements children of all times and all places have needed to be healthy and happy, such as food, clothing, fun, chores, and love.

Lesson 4: **Then and Now** (Grades 1–6; one class period)

Students compare the life of the child in the central story with their lives to see the different ways in which children meet each of their needs.

Lesson 5: **Then and Now Books** (Grades 1–3; two to three class periods)

Using charts from Lessons 3 and 4, students write individual books telling and illustrating the differences between children living in times before ours and children living now.

Lesson 6: **Artifacts** (Grades 1–6; one class period)

Students learn how to make inferences about a culture based on common, everyday artifacts from a teacher's home.

Lesson 7: **Artifacts Homework** (Grades 1–6; one class period)

Students bring three artifacts from home for others to make inferences about.

Lesson 8: **Grandparents' Childhood** (Grades 1–6; one class period)

Students interview grandparents (or older people who visit the school) for details about their childhood, including artifacts that they would have brought to school.

Lesson 9: **Artifacts Field Trip** (Grades 1–6; 1/2 to 1 day)

Students visit a museum to study artifacts and to record their own inferences about what the artifacts reveal about former cultures.

Lesson 10: **Comparing Music** (Grades 1–6; variable)

Students explore music from various cultures and compare music's place in other cultures contrasted with the place of music in their own lives.

Lesson 11: **Toys and Games** (Grades 1–6; variable)

Students make and learn to play games from other times and other cultures.

Synopsis of When I Was Young in the Mountains

When I Was Young in the Mountains is a picture book that lovingly reflects on the author's childhood in Appalachia. The writer recalls various details of her life, including the old general store, the little schoolhouse that doubled as a church on Sunday, and the muddy swimming hole.

Explanation of Unit Focus: Needs of Children through Time and Space

This unit is meant to develop an attitude of acceptance and understanding of the practices and preferences of various cultures by helping students think about the basic similarities among us all. By asking students to consider the various ways in which all children meet their basic human needs, commonalities become more important than differences. This theme gives us an incentive to motivate our students to read books about children from other times and other places.

Cross-Curricular Connections

You might link to your science curriculum to explore and research some of the inventions that so changed our world. You could look up the inventions as a class or have each student research a different modern invention and report to the class.

To Start the Unit

Look at the suggested lessons and select those that are appropriate for your class. Read *When I Was Young in the Mountains* aloud to your students, then proceed with any lesson you choose.

Literature Connections

Following is a list of books on the unit's focus for your students to read independently during the unit and even after you have finished the unit. If each student is reading a different book, discussions and activities regarding the unit's focus will be far richer than if everyone reads the same selection. See technique 1, Free Reading with Literature Connections, for suggestions.

Picture Books

Allen, Thomas. 1989. *On Grandaddy's Farm.* Knopf.
Ashley, Bernard. 1991. *Cleversticks.* Crown.
Baylor, Byrd. 1983. *Best Town in the World.* Scribner.
Brodsky, Beverly. 1979. *Secret Places.* Lippincott.
Clifford, Eth. 1985. *The Remembering Box.* Houghton Mifflin.
Gilman, Phoebe. 1993. *Something from Nothing.* Scholastic.
Grifalconi, Ann. 1986. *Village of Round and Square Houses.* Little.
Griffith, Helen. 1987. *Grandaddy's Place.* Greenwillow.
Hazen, Barbara. 1979. *Tight Times.* Puffin.
Hendershot, Judith. 1993. *Up the Track to Grandma's.* Knopf.
Isadora, Rachel. 1991. *At the Crossroads.* Greenwillow.
Johnston, Tony. 1985. *The Quilt Story.* Putnam.
Kroll, Virginia. 1992. *Masai and I.* Four Winds.
Levine, Ellen. 1989. *I Hate English.* Scholastic.
Levinson, Riki. 1985. *Watch the Stars Come Out.* Dutton.
———. 1986. *I Go with my Family to Grandma's.* Dutton.
McCloskey, Robert. 1957. *Time of Wonder.* Viking.
McDonald, Megan. 1992. *Great Pumpkin Switch.* Orchard.
McLerran, Alice. 1991. *Roxaboxen.* Lothrop.
Pedersen, Judy. 1991. *Out in the Country.* Knopf.
Purdy, Carol. 1987. *Least of All.* McElderry.
Reiser, Joanne. 1983. *Hannah's Alaska.* Raintree.
Rylant, Cynthia. 1985. *The Relatives Came.* Brabury.
———. 1992. *Birthday Presents.* Orchard.
Sandin, Joan. 1981. *The Long Way to a New Land.* Harper and Row.
Schroeder, Alan. 1989. *Ragtime Tumpie.* Little.
Stevenson, James. 1992. *Don't You Know There's a War On?* Greenwillow.
Trivias, Irene. 1992. *Annie . . . Anya.* Orchard.
Turner, Ann. 1985. *Dakota Dugout.* Macmillan.
Van Leeuwen, Jean. 1992. *Going West.* Dial.
Wild, Margaret, and Julie Vivas. 1991. *Let the Celebration Begin!* Orchard.
Williams, Karen Lynn. 1991. *When Africa Was Home.* Orchard.
Williams, Vera. 1982. *A Chair for My Mother.* Greenwillow.
Yolen, Jane. 1992. *Letting Swift River Go.* Little.
Zeifert, Harriet. 1986. *A New Coat for Anna.* Knopf.
Zolotow, Charlotte. 1963. *The Sky Was Blue.* Harper.

Longer Books

Baker, Betty. 1963. *Killer-of-Death.* Harper.

Blos, Joan. 1979. *Gathering of Days.* Scribner.

Brink, Carol. 1962. *Caddie Woodlawn.* Aladdin Books.

Burnett, Frances H. 1990. *The Secret Garden.* Dell.

Byars, Betsy. 1977. *Pinballs.* Harper.

Fritz, Jean. 1982. *Homesick.* Putnam.

Gates, Doris. 1940. *Blue Willow.* Viking.

Gray, Elizabeth. 1942. *Adam of the Road.* Viking Children's Books.

Hamilton, Virginia. 1967. *Zeely.* Macmillan.

Hanson, Joyce. 1980. *Gift-Giver.* Houghton Mifflin.

Krumgold, Joseph. 1987. *And Now, Miguel.* HarperCollins Children's Books.

Kurelek, William. 1975. *Prairie Boy's Summer.* Tundra Books.

Lindquist, Jennie. 1955. *Golden Name Day.* Harper.

Lord, Bette Bao. 1984. *In the Year of the Boar and Jackie Robinson.* Harper.

Lowry, Lois. 1989. *Number the Stars.* Houghton Mifflin.

MacLachlan, Patricia. 1985. *Sarah, Plain and Tall.* Harper.

Montgomery, L. M. 1988. *Anne of Green Gables.* Doubleday.

O'Dell, Scott. 1990. *Island of the Blue Dolphins.* Houghton Mifflin.

Orlov, Uri. 1984. *Island on Bird Street.* Houghton Mifflin.

Pitts, Paul. 1988. *Racing the Sun.* Avon.

Rogers, Jean. 1990. *Trading Game.* Harper.

Slote, Alfred. 1990. *Trading Game.* Harper.

Spinelli, Jerry. 1992. *Maniac McGee.* HarperCollins Children's Books.

Taylor, Sydney. 1966. *All-of-a-Kind Family.* Dell.

Uchida, Yoshiko. 1971. *Journey to Topaz.* Scribner.

Warner, Gertrude Chandler. 1967. *The Boxcar Children.* A. Whitman. (Other books in this series are also appropriate.)

Wilder, Laura Ingalls. 1953. *Little House on the Prairie.* Harper.

Yep, Laurence. 1977. *Child of the Owl.* Harper.

Lesson 1

FREE READING WITH LITERATURE CONNECTIONS

Materials

books from the literature connections list or any other books about common needs of children all over the world

Preparation

Gather a variety of books of different lengths and different reading levels that address the unit focus (see Literature Connections, page 134, for suggestions).

Procedure

Have students read freely in self-directed books for an extended period each day and report on their reading to the class. See technique 1, page 267.

Multiple Intelligence Connections

Lesson 2

FAVORITE READ-ALOUDS

Materials

read-aloud books from literature connections or other books about children's needs throughout time

Preparation

Photocopy the cover or title page, whichever has a more interesting picture, of each day's read-aloud selection.

Procedure

Read aloud to your class at least one story a day from your unit-oriented collection. After about a week, have students vote on their favorite books. See technique 2, Read-Alouds, page 268 for details.

Multiple Intelligence Connections

COMMON NEEDS

Materials

sheet of chart paper

felt-tip pens

Preparation

Read *When I Was Young in the Mountains*.

Procedure

Step 1: Tell students that they will be working on a unit about common needs of children through time and all over the world. Ask each student to write down the basic needs that we have in common with the children in *When I Was Young in the Mountains*. Ask "What have children throughout all time and all over the world needed for health and happiness?"

Step 2: Ask students to share their lists with study partners and merge their lists into one. For accountability, ask partners to sign their names on their composite lists and turn them in.

Step 3: Label the chart paper "Common Needs of All Children for Health and Happiness." (For first grade you might shorten it to "Common Needs.")

Step 4: Ask students to raise their hands and share their lists with you as you record on the graph paper all of the class's ideas. Do not record the same idea twice. Try to reframe suggestions in a way that allows all children to relate to them. If someone says, "mother and father," suggest "family." If someone says "church," suggest "beliefs." This list will be used for several future lessons, so print it legibly and leave it posted in a prominent location. As you work in some of the future lessons, you may find other needs to add, such as music and exercise, which aren't mentioned in our central book. Following are some examples:

Food	*Fun*
Clothing	*Protection from danger*
Shelter	*Light*
Family	*Love*
Friends	*Warmth*
Toys	*Chores and a sense of*
Learning	*being needed to help out*

Step 5: Proceed directly to lesson 4 for the appropriate grade.

Multiple Intelligence Connections

Lesson 4

THEN AND NOW

Materials

chart of common needs from lesson 3

two additional sheets of chart paper

felt-tip pens

Preparation

Do lesson 3. Add two more sheets to the right of lesson 3's chart of common needs, labeling the second chart "then" and the third, "now."

Procedure

Step 1: With the class, read over the list on the chart of common needs. Then reread *When I Was Young in the Mountains*, asking students to stop you whenever they hear one of the ways that the children in that story met one of the needs listed on your chart. Record the need on the appropriate chart (see example below).

Food

Then	Now
cornbread, pinto beans, and fried okra	

Step 2: After you record each idea on the "Then" chart, ask how that need is met by most children in our country now. Add that comment on the "Now" chart directly across from the "Then" entry (see example below). Keep in mind that you are listing things that children need to be healthy and happy, not everything they could possibly desire.

Food

Then	Now
cornbread, pinto beans, and fried okra	Pizza, hamburgers, tacos

Step 3: When the story is completed, the chart should be complete, as well. Read the charts over together and talk about the changes between then and now. Leave the charts posted during the remainder of this unit, as you will refer to them in other activities.

Step 4: Do lesson 5 the next school day.

Multiple Intelligence Connections

Lesson 5

THEN AND NOW BOOKS

Materials

charts of common needs from lessons 3 and 4

teacher-made books

Preparation

Do lessons 3 and 4. Make books for students using eight lined sheets on bottom and eight blank sheets on top (see technique 5, Teacher-Made Books, page 273).

Procedure

Step 1: On a transparency or chalkboard, model for students how to write a set of pages in their books. The two facing story pages will always contrast how children in stories about the past met their needs with how they meet their needs now (see example below).

Step 2: Students begin work in their individual books, selecting any of the ideas from the class charts. To ensure adherence to spelling and writing conventions, tell students to raise their hands when they reach the end of each page. Look at each page. If there are mistakes, ask such questions as, "Which of these words is spelled wrong?" "Which word needs a capital letter?" "How do I know this sentence is finished?" (metacognition).

Step 3: After you check the printing, help with corrections, and put an official teacher mark on each page, students may illustrate their work. With this correct-as-you-go process, you do not need to collect and correct the work, and students learn the skills they need during a meaningful process.

Step 4: Over the next several work periods, students continue to add other ideas from the class charts to each set of pages until the books are complete.

Step 5: Have students select their best pages for a special stamp or sticker. Photocopy those pages and put them in the students' portfolios.

Step 6: Read a few pages from each book aloud to the class or have students read their books to five or more classmates. Let students sign the backs of all the books that are read to them and send the books home.

More Challenge

Students might choose one of the other books from the literature connections list on page 134 to make a second book, comparing their lives to those of children in yet another time and place.

Multiple Intelligence Connections

ARTIFACTS

Materials for Each Student

a copy of work sheet 6-1, Artifacts, cut into half sheets

a pencil

Materials for the Teacher

four items from your home that tell something about the kind of person you are, for example, a bookmark, a trowel, a recipe collection, a bike

an overhead transparency of work sheet 6-1, Artifacts

Preparation

Bring four artifacts from home that match a variety of needs such as one for chores, one for fun, one for food, one for learning. Photocopy enough copies of work sheet 6-1 to provide each student with three half-sheets for the three descriptions. Make an overhead transparency of work sheet 6-1 for yourself.

Procedure

Step 1: Tell students that one of the ways we find out about how people have met their needs in other times and in other places is to study what they have left behind. These items are called *artifacts*. Artifacts are something that people make and use (not a natural item, such as a rock). When archaeologists find an artifact such as a bow and arrow or a woven basket, that item tells them something about the people who made and used it. Invite students to tell you what the discovery of a bow and arrow would tell us about a people; then do the same with the woven basket.

Step 2: Tell students that the same is true today. A few artifacts that someone owns reveals a lot about that person. Show students the artifacts from your home and invite them to act as archaeologists and make inferences about what your home life is like.

Step 3: Give students pencils and three copies of work sheet 6-1 and challenge them to write their inferences about how you spend your time at home. Then, using one of your artifacts and the overhead transparency of work sheet 6-1, demonstrate how to complete the work sheet. After you discuss the item and model the drawing and writing, students are more likely to understand and do a thorough and creative job on their own.

Step 4: Students draw each artifact on work sheet 6-1 and then talk with a study partner about what that artifact reveals about their teacher's life at home.

Step 5: After a short discussion period, students record their ideas on their own work sheets.

Additional Step for Grades 1 and 2

- Create a simpler work sheet as needed and ask students to draw the artifact, discuss it with a partner, and together write their inferences about how the teacher spends some of his or her free time.

More Challenge

Step 1: After students have finished work sheet 6-1, ask them to imagine that they are living several hundred years in the future and that these artifacts have been found in an archaeological dig. In addition to drawing the artifact, they must describe it in detail, as if they were seeing it from a long time in the future.

Step 2: Students write their inferences about the life of the person who owned this artifact, again as if they were living far in the future and making their best guesses about the life of a person in the twentieth century.

Step 3: At the bottom of the paper, students identify which of the needs from the lesson 3 chart have been met with this artifact. It will still be helpful at this level of greater challenge to model the entire process with one of the artifacts before students begin their work on the remaining three.

Multiple Intelligence Connections

ARTIFACTS HOMEWORK

Materials

pencils

work sheet 6-1, Artifacts

parent note 6-1

three items students bring from home as artifacts

Preparation

Do lesson 7. Duplicate enough copies of work sheet 6-1 to provide three half-sheets for each student. Also make a copy of parent note 6-1 for each student after you add any limits that you want to impose for the safety of the items and the maintenance of order in your classroom.

Procedure

Step 1: Ask students to bring three of their own artifacts to school the next day. Ask them to bring no more than one toy so that you get a variety of artifacts. Set whatever other limits you need to set such as limits on toy weapons or on size or value.

Step 2: After you and your students brainstorm and record some items that might tell others interesting aspects of students' lives, suggest they write some of these ideas in their individual homework notes. Tell students that even a small and seemingly unimportant artifact, such as a fork, audiotape, or a button, can tell a great deal.

If you think bringing actual artifacts will be potentially troublesome, have students draw pictures of their three artifacts instead.

Step 3: Send parent note 6-1 home for homework, modifying it for pictures instead of actual artifacts if you prefer.

Step 4: Repeat the procedure you followed in lesson 7 using work sheet 6-1 or a simpler version for grades 1 and 2, except that this time students will pair up and write about their partners' artifacts. No questions are allowed. Students who forgot their homework can draw the three artifacts they would have brought, and the pictures can be used in place of the actual artifacts.

Step 5: Just before students hand in their papers, have them write on the backs to tell you their thoughts and feelings about this project. Ask them to reflect about what made it fun or not, easy or difficult (metacognition).

Step 6: On the same day, do lesson 10.

Multiple Intelligence Connections

Lesson 8

GRANDPARENTS' CHILDHOOD

Materials

copies of work sheet 6-2, Grandparents' Childhood

copies of parent note 6-2

Preparation

Duplicate parent note 6-2. (For first and second grade add a line to tell parents that they can do the printing for their students if necessary.) Find someone aged 60 or older who can be interviewed by your class, and ask her or him to think of three artifacts from her or his childhood that would reveal something about life in those times.

Procedure

Step 1: Tell students that they are going to be studying artifacts that reveal the history of their own families. Discuss how they think their grandparent's childhoods were different from theirs.

Step 2: Read the note from work sheet 6-2 with your class, discuss it, and send it home for homework. Tell students that if for any reason they cannot get enough information at home they will be able to interview someone their grandparents' age at school the next day. (Students should not be penalized for not getting the information. Some may not have living grandparents or may not be able to talk to their grandparents. Other grandparents may simply not wish to answer the questions.)

Step 3: At the beginning of the period, introduce the "grandparents" you have found and ask them to tell the class about artifacts that would tell a lot about the times of their childhoods. You may even be able to find someone who has some artifacts, such as a doll or other toy, a photograph, an article of clothing, a favorite book, a record, to bring.

Step 4: When the grandparents leave, ask students to take out their homework if they have been able to do it, and look over the information that they have gathered.

Step 5: Divide the class into two groups, those who did the homework and those who did not or could not. Have those who did the homework pair up and share their information with each other. Those who did not do the homework can do it now, based on the classroom interview with the grandparent.

Step 6: As both groups finish, they can turn their homework papers over and answer these two questions:

> *If you could go back in time, why might you like to be a child in your grandparents' days?*
>
> *What things do you think you would miss the most?*

Multiple Intelligence Connections

Lesson 9

ARTIFACTS FIELD TRIP

Prerequisite

Do lesson 8.

Materials for Each Student

a permission slip
other items required for a field trip
a pencil
clipboard
a copy of work sheet 6-1, Artifacts

Preparation

Arrange for a class field trip to a museum where you will find artifacts of another culture. For example, visit a wild west museum, a restored fort or American Indian village, a historic home, or a historical museum. Duplicate enough copies of work sheet 6-1 as you would like your students to use at the museum.

Procedure

Step 1: Let students know that they will be visiting a museum to learn from the artifacts they will find there.

Step 2: Give each student a pencil, several half-sheets of work sheet 6-1, and a clipboard. Before leaving the classroom, remind students how to use work sheet 6-1 to report on an artifact.

Step 3: At the museum, in addition to other activities you select to do with your students, give them at least one-half hour to select their own artifacts to draw and write about. You may wish to limit their choices to certain areas of the museum and assign assistants to help your groups.

Step 4: Back at the classroom, let students share their work either by showing and explaining it to partners or by using the guessing game from lesson 9.

Step 5: Give students fresh sheets of lined paper to tell what they have learned about the importance of the study of artifacts, both from their work at school and at the museum (metacognition).

Multiple Intelligence Connections

COMPARING MUSIC

Materials

records

tapes

sheet music

musicians to access music of other times and other places

Preparation

Search for music that correlates with the reading that your students are doing on this unit's focus.

Procedure

Step 1: Talk to students about the part music has played in every culture. You might like to brainstorm a list of musical instruments that people have played over the centuries.

Step 2: Bring in music that represents a variety of cultures. For *When I Was Young in the Mountains,* for example, you could play recordings of bluegrass music, search for a fiddler or other country musician to play for your students, find a caller to teach square dance or contra dance, teach them some old popular tunes such as "Pop Goes the Weasel," "Blue Tail Fly," "Oh, Susannah," "Old Joe Clark," or "You Are My Sunshine."

Step 3: After students have learned or listened to some music from other times and places, use work sheet 6-3, Venn Diagram, to help students compare why music is important to them personally now and why they think it has always been important to people as a group. Do this activity with the whole class so that thinking is stimulated by everyone's ideas. To ensure full participation, you might require that all students fill in their copy of the class diagram using work sheet 6-3 (see example on page 148).

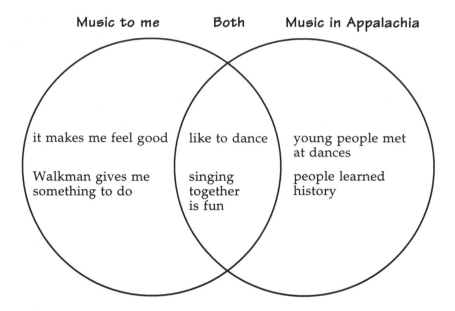

Music to me   Both   Music in Appalachia

it makes me feel good   like to dance   young people met at dances

Walkman gives me something to do   singing together is fun   people learned history

Additional Step for Grades 3 through 6

- Ask students to write a paragraph or two telling their thoughts and feelings about the ideas discussed in the Venn diagram. You might have students write letters to their parents telling what they learned about music. They could take the letters home along with their copies of the Venn diagram.

Multiple Intelligence Connections

Lesson 11   TOYS AND GAMES

Materials

books and/or people to teach students how to make games and toys from other times and places

Preparation

Seek sources that can teach your students to make or play the games and toys that are mentioned in the literature connection books that they are reading. Gather necessary materials.

Procedure

Step 1: Visit your librarian or local teachers' store to locate books that tell students how to make and play games from other cultures and other times. I highly recommend cat's cradle, the string game. It fascinates students from first through sixth; there are many books out now that show how to do it. Games for older children, such as marbles and jacks, can be captivating as well. Then there are games from other countries.

Step 2: Choose some of these games to make and play with your students. You might have the whole class work together on a project such as learning cat's cradle or learning to play marbles or jacks. Or you might list several toys that students might make and let students form groups according to their interest.

Adding Metacognition

If students work on this project over the course of several days, you could have them use work sheet 6-4, Intentions and Reflections, to keep track of their progress and their successes. See technique 7, Intentions and Reflections, for further information about this process.

Unit
6

MATERIALS

Work Sheet 6-1 — Artifacts

Draw:

Description: _____
_____
_____

Function: _____
_____
_____

Inference about owner: _____
_____
_____
_____

Need met by artifact: _____
_____

- -

Draw:

Description: _____
_____
_____

Function: _____
_____
_____

Inference about owner: _____
_____
_____
_____

Need met by artifact: _____
_____

Dear Parents,

As part of our literature unit on the needs of children all over the world, we are studying about artifacts. Artifacts are any items that people make and use, and artifacts from other times and places can teach us a great deal about how those people lived their lives and met their human needs. Would you please help your child select three items that reveal something about his or her interests and send them to school tomorrow? Some possibilities are an audiotape, a toy, a food wrapper, a tool your child uses, a special item of clothing such as a ski cap, a ticket from a show, an item from a collection, a favorite book. Where possible, record your child's name on the artifact.

Although we will take good care of the artifacts, please do not send anything that cannot be replaced if an accident should happen. The items will be sent back home tomorrow.

Please do not send _____

_____

Thank you,

Work Sheet 6-2
Grandparents' Childhood

1. How were your toys different from my toys?

_____
_____
_____
_____
_____

2. How was food prepared then?

_____
_____
_____
_____
_____

3. How were clothes different? What did you wear to school when you were my age?

_____
_____
_____
_____
_____

4. (Explain your artifact homework.) If you had to bring three artifacts to school when you were my age, what would they have been?

_____
_____
_____
_____
_____

5. What do you think were the best things about your childhood?

_____
_____
_____
_____
_____

Dear Parent(s),

As part of our unit about children's lives in other times and other places, I would like to ask for your help with a homework assignment. I have asked your child to ask a grandparent the questions below and to write those answers down and bring them to school tomorrow. If it is possible for your child to talk with a grandparent, or if you could supply the answers from your own knowledge of his or her life, tomorrow's assignment will have a uniquely personal value.

If for any reason there is not an available grandparent or you do not wish to participate in this assignment, we will have a grandparent to interview at school tomorrow and your child will not be marked down or miss out on any of the value of the lesson.

Thank you for your help,

Work Sheet 6-3

Venn Diagram

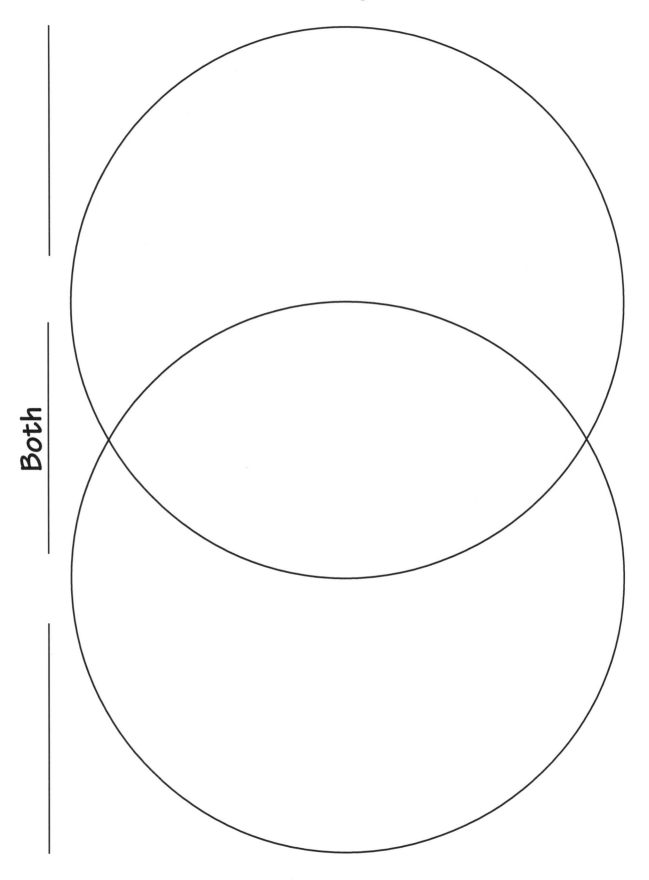

Both

Work Sheet 6-4
Intentions and Reflections
Adding Metacognition to Projects

Date:_____ Today I intend to _____

_____

_____

_____

_____

During this work period, I was able to _____

_____

_____

Tomorrow I hope to

_____

_____

- -

Date:_____ Today I intend to _____

_____

_____

_____

_____

During this work period, I was able to _____

_____

_____

Tomorrow I hope to

_____

_____

- -

Note: For longer projects use additional sheets or have students use a teacher-made journal to make similar daily entries.

Unit 7

OVERVIEW

Central Literature Selection:
Pig Pig Grows Up
by David McPhail

Unit Focus:
Milestones in Growing Up
Grades: 1–6

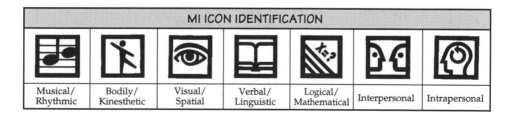

THINKING SKILLS SYMBOLS IDENTIFICATION				
Personal Connection	Creation	Mastery	Reasoning	Metacognition

MI ICON IDENTIFICATION						
Musical/ Rhythmic	Bodily/ Kinesthetic	Visual/ Spatial	Verbal/ Linguistic	Logical/ Mathematical	Interpersonal	Intrapersonal

Lesson 1: **Free Reading with Literature Connections** (Grades 1–6; twenty minutes a day)

Students keep track of unit focus books that are read aloud and vote weekly on their favorites.

Lesson 2: **Favorite Read-Alouds** (Grades 1–3; five to ten minutes a day)

Keep track of all read-alouds that match the unit; let students vote on favorite.

Lesson 3: **Growing-up Books** (Grades 1–4; five to eight class periods)

Student-made books with pictures and text about milestones for each year of their lives so far.

Lesson 4: **Alike and Different** (Grades 1–3; one to two class periods)

Students analyze similarities and differences between Pig Pig and Peter Pan.

Lesson 5: **Sequencing** (Grades 1–4; two to three class periods)

Students learn sequencing by creating a bulletin board; each student copies the text from one page of *Pig Pig Grows Up* and illustrates it.

Lesson 6: **Plan and Perform the Story** (Grades 1–6; three to five class periods and a performance)

Students are guided to decide on a creative format for performing Pig Pig's story and practice metacognition by keeping track of daily goals and self-assessing.

Lesson 7: **Parent Interview** (Grades 1–6; one to two class periods and homework)

Students interview a parent for a growing-up story that they share with the class in a creative way.

Lesson 8: **Plus and Minus** (Grades 3–6; one to two class periods)

Students practice writing an opinion paper after exploring the positive and negative aspects of growing up.

Lesson 9: **Imagine an Ending to a Greek Myth** (Grades 5–6; one period)

Students build comprehension skills by imagining a new ending to the Greek myth of Phaeton and Apollo, a classic growing-up adventure.

Lesson 10: **Venn Diagrams** (Grades 5–6; one period)

Students use Venn diagrams to analyze and compare two characters thoughtfully.

Synopsis of *Pig Pig Grows Up*

Pig Pig Grows Up is a delightful picture book about a rather big young pig who absolutely refuses to grow up until . . . his quick action saves a real baby and changes his opinion about taking responsibility. Although *Pig Pig Grows Up* is a short picture book, its appeal to all ages from kindergarten to adult makes it a perfect focus for a unit that spans all of the elementary grade levels. Intermediate grade students love an occasional picture book, and this one will amuse, entertain, and stimulate thinking about their own growing up. An advantage to building a unit on a picture book, a short story, a poem, or a song is that you can dive right into the activities without having to adjust your lessons to the reading of a lengthy chapter book.

Explanation of Unit Focus: Milestones in Growing Up

Students will be thinking about the joys and pains of growing up, a topic that stimulates thought in children of all ages. There is such a desire to grow up and be able to do grown-up things, and yet a reluctance to let go of the pleasures and relative shelter of childhood. This unit will invite students to explore their experiences and their feelings about the growing up they have done and the growing up they have yet to do.

Cross-Curricular Connections

You might time this unit to coincide with family life education or anti-drug education at any grade level, emphasizing how choices and responsibilities increase as we grow older. A science unit related to human growth also correlates well with this unit.

To Start the Unit

Look at the suggested lessons and select those that are appropriate for your class. Read *Pig Pig Grows Up* aloud to your students, then proceed with any lesson you choose.

Literature Connections

Here is a list of books on the unit's focus for your students to read independently during the unit and even after you have finished the unit. If each student is reading a different book, discussions and activities regarding the unit's focus will be far richer than if everyone reads the same selection. See technique 1, Free Reading with Literature Connections, for suggestions.

Primary Books

Birdseye, Tom. 1988. *Airmail to the Moon*. Holiday.

Brown, Marc. 1988. *D. W. All Wet*. Little.

Browne, Anthony. 1986. *The Piggybook*. Knopf.

Bunting, Eve. 1990. *The Wall*. Clarion.

Carrick, Carol, and Donald Carrick. 1975. *Old Mother Witch*. Clarion.

Cooney, Barbara. 1982. *Miss Rumphius*. Viking.

Fiday, Beverly. 1990. *Time to Go*. Harcourt Brace.

Gauch, Patricia. 1987. *Christina Katerina and the Time She Quit the Family*. Putnam.

Giff, Patricia. 1993. *Next Year I'll Be Special*. Doubleday.

Grifalconi, Ann. 1990. *Osa's Pride*. Little.

Henkes, Kevin. 1990. *Julius, the Baby of the World*. Greenwillow.

Hoban, Lillian. 1974. *Arthur's Honey Bear*. Harper.

Keats, Ezra Jack. 1964. *A Whistle for Willie*. Viking.

Kraus, Robert. 1987. *Owliver*. Simon & Schuster.

McPhail, David. 1976. *Henry Bear's Park*. Little, Brown.

Ness, Evaline. 1966. *Sam, Bangs and Moonshine*. Holt.

Noll, Sally. 1991. *That Bothered Kate*. Greenwillow.

Peter Pan, any version

Polacco, Patricia. 1990. *Babushka's Doll*. Simon & Schuster.

Row, Eileen. 1990. *All I Am*. Macmillan.

Schwartz, Amy. 1988. *Anabelle Swift, Kindergartner*. Orchard.

Shapiro, Arnold. 1987. *What Can I Dream About?* Price.

Viorst, Judith. 1976. *Alexander and the Terrible, Horrible, No Good, Very Bad Day*. Atheneum.

Waber, Bernard. 1975. *Ira Sleeps Over*. Houghton Mifflin.

Ward, Lynd. 1952. *The Biggest Bear*. Houghton Mifflin.

Weiss, Nicki. 1982. *Hank and Oogie*. Greenwillow.

Wells, Rosemary. 1993. *Waiting for the Evening Star*. Dial.

Wood, Audrey. 1990. *Oh My Baby Bear*. Harcourt Brace.

Yolen, Jane. 1991. *All Those Secrets of the World*. Little.

Zolotow, Charlotte. 1971. *A Father Like That*. Harper.

Longer Books

Babbitt, Natalie. 1985. *Tuck Everlasting.* Farrar, Straus and Giroux.

Banks, Lynne Reid. 1992. *One More River.* Morrow.

Birdseye, Tom. 1990. *Tucker.* Holiday.

Blume, Judy. 1972. *Otherwise Known as Sheila the Great.* Dutton.

Brady, Esther Wood. 1993. *Toliver's Secret.* Random Books for Young Readers.

Brink, Carol Ryrie. 1972. *Bad Times of Irma Baumlein.* Macmillan.

Cleary, Beverly. 1972. *Ramona and Her Father.* Morrow.

Eckert, Allan W. 1971. *Incident at Hawk's Hill.* Little, Brown.

Fleischman, Sid. 1986. *The Whipping Boy.* Greenwillow.

Little, Jean. 1986. *Different Dragons.* Viking Kestrel.

MacLachlan, Patricia. 1988. *The Facts and Fictions of Minna Pratt.* Harper.

Miles, Miska. 1972. *Annie and the Old One.* Little.

Pascal, Francine. 1991. *Hangin' Out with Cici.* Puffin.

Paterson, Katherine. 1978. *The Great Gilly Hopkins.* Harper.

Paulsen, Gary. 1987. *Hatchet.* Bradbury.

Pitts, Paul. 1988. *Racing the Sun.* Avon.

Rylant, Cynthia. 1992. *Missing May.* Orchard.

Shreve, Norma. 1979. *Family Secrets.* Knopf.

Smith, Robert Kimmel. 1984. *War with Grandpa.* Delacorte.

Speare, Elizabeth. 1983. *The Sign of the Beaver.* Houghton Mifflin.

Taylor, Theodore. 1969. *The Cay.* Doubleday.

FREE READING WITH LITERATURE CONNECTIONS

Materials

books from literature connections or any other books that focus on growing up

Preparation

Gather books on the unit's focus of growing up. They can be of various reading levels so that every student can find something he or she is comfortable reading (see Literature Connections, page 160, for suggestions).

Procedure

Have students read freely in self-selected books for an extended period each day. Also have them report on their reading to the class. See technique 1, Free Reading with Literature Connections, on page 267 for more information.

Multiple Intelligence Connections

FAVORITE READ-ALOUDS

Materials

read-aloud books from literature connections or other books about growing up

Preparation

Photocopy the cover or title page, whichever has a more interesting picture, of each day's read-aloud selection.

Procedure

Read aloud to your class at least one story a day from your unit-oriented collection. After about a week, have students vote on their favorites. See technique 2, Read-Alouds, on page 268 for details.

Multiple Intelligence Connections

GROWING-UP BOOKS

Materials

teacher-made books
writing paper
pencils
crayons or felt-tip pens

Preparation

Make a book for each student by alternating half-sheets of drawing paper with half-sheets of lined paper. See page 273 for instructions. Students will need one set of pages for every year of their age.

Procedure

Step 1: Read or reread *Pig Pig Grows Up* and discuss the turning points that make us feel grown-up.

Step 2: Relate an incident from your life that let you know you were growing up. (It is best if the event occurred when you were about the same age as your students are now.)

Step 3: Brainstorm together about happy incidents in students' lives that let them know they were growing up (losing teeth, walking to the store, first day of school, reaching the sink without a stool, joining little league, and others). As students tell you all of their ideas, write them on the board for all to see. For grades 3 through 4, first ask students to make individual lists of three or four growing-up events. Then ask them to read their lists to study partners, adding any new ideas that they think of together.

Step 4: Ask students to number down the left edge of a sheet of paper from 1 to their current age, and try to remember and record something that they did at each age. There will probably be some blanks (see example below).

1

2 *rode a trike*

3

4 *could reach the bathroom sink*

5 *first day of kindergarten*

Step 5: Either work with the whole class to help students think of things they might have done during the years for which they have no entries, or assign that task for homework so that parents can help them think of what they might have done to mark growing up each year.

Step 6: After students have completed their lists and you have checked them for correct spelling and punctuation, give out the teacher-made books and shown how to record and illustrate one year's growth on each page (see example below). This step may take several work periods.

When I was one, I learned to stand up.

Step 7: When they are finished, have students read their books to each other, signing the backs of all books that are read to them, and then take their books home to parents with parent note 7-1.

More Challenge

Students write each page in rhyme. Start by brainstorming words that rhyme with the number words for each age (*one: fun, run, done, sun, begun*) and give them the first phrase of the sentence (see example below).

> **You provide the following phrase:**
> *When I was only one . . .*
> **Students create the rest:**
> *I could walk, and that was fun* or *I could walk and run*
> **You provide the following phrase:**
> *When I was only two . . .*
> **Students create the rest:**
> *I learned to tie my shoe* or *I dressed myself in blue*

Multiple Intelligence Connections

Lesson 4

ALIKE AND DIFFERENT

Materials

story paper for primary grades

work sheet 7-1, Venn Diagram

pencils

Preparation

Make an overhead transparency of work sheet 7-1 to record students' input or draw a large Venn diagram on chart paper. Label one circle Peter Pan and one circle Pig Pig.

Procedure

Step 1: As a class, read *Pig Pig Grows Up* and a picture-book version of *Peter Pan*.

Step 2: Ask students to tell some ways that Peter Pan and Pig Pig are alike, such as they don't want to grow up. As soon as someone gives you an idea, write it in the overlapping area of the two Venn diagram circles. Give hints.

Step 3: Ask students to tell you some ways in which Pig Pig is different from Peter Pan. Record these ideas in the Pig Pig–only circle. Give hints.

Step 4: Ask for ways that Peter Pan is different from Pig Pig and record these in Peter's circle.

Step 5: With the class reading aloud with you, reread all of the class's ideas.

Step 6: Give students story paper and a choice of two frame sentences. They can choose either

Pig Pig _____

but Peter Pan_____

or

Pig Pig and Peter Pan both _____

_____

Step 7: Tell students to pick one of the sentences and use the phrases from the Venn diagram to complete it. Students can write and illustrate their sentences on the story paper.

Step 8: When papers are complete, collect and bind them into a class book. Read the book aloud, acknowledging authors, and add it to your class library.

More Challenge

Instead of steps 6 and 7, either let students compose their own "alike" or "different" sentences using the ideas from the Venn diagram, or give them the choice of these frame sentences:

Pig Pig and Peter Pan are different because Pig Pig _____

_____

and Peter Pan _____

or

Pig Pig and Peter Pan are alike in some ways, because they both

_____

_____

Tell students to write and illustrate their own sentences on story paper and read them to you as soon as they are done with the writing portion. You can help students with correct spelling and conventions during the writing process, since others will read these sentences.

Multiple Intelligence Connections

Lesson 5

SEQUENCING

Materials for Each Student

drawing paper

felt-tip pens or crayons

Preparation

Have the text of *Pig Pig Grows Up* available for students to copy onto their sentence strips. Also see technique 9, Visualization, on page 280 for helpful information.

Procedure

Step 1: Reread *Pig Pig Grows Up*, this time without showing the illustrations. At the end of each page, stop and ask five or six students to tell you in some detail what they see happening in their minds' eyes. Press for detail to help your students learn how to bring a story fully to life with their own imaginations. Ask questions such as the following:

What is Pig Pig wearing?

What color is his blanket?

Is he sitting, standing, or what?

Is he in the house or outside?

What kind of a road is his stroller rolling over?

Step 2: Before reading the next page, invite one student to draw the picture that he or she just described. Give that volunteer art paper, a sentence strip, and a copy of the first page's text. Tell the child to draw first, while the mental picture is fresh and clear, and then to copy the text. (In first grade, you might give them photocopied text to paste to their pictures.)

Step 3: Proceed in the same way: Read one page at a time, discuss mental images, select one student to illustrate the page, and send that student to begin drawing immediately while you continue to read with the rest of the class.

Step 4: When all pages have been assigned, you may have a few students left over, depending on the size of your class. These students can help you prepare an empty bulletin board for the pictures the other students are drawing. You will need the following items:

letters for the title of the book

letters for the author

optional: a border around the edge of the bulletin board

Step 5: When all pictures and text are finished, call the class to attention and ask which child thinks he or she has the first picture.

Step 6: When a hand raises, let the child show his or her picture and read the text. If the class agrees that this picture is first, pin picture with text on the bulletin board in the first position.

Step 7: Continue in this fashion, asking who thinks he or she has the next picture, having that child explain the content; ask for class consensus and pin the picture and text to the bulletin board.

Step 8: When all pictures and text are up on the bulletin board, have the class read the story aloud with you. Add a long string of yarn from picture to picture so that students can follow it to practice reading the story on their own.

Multiple Intelligence Connections

Lesson 6

PLAN AND PERFORM THE STORY

Materials

whatever students need to make puppets, scenery, or anything else for their performances

Preparation

Read or reread *Pig Pig Grows Up*.

Procedure

Step 1: With your students decide on a format to rehearse and present this story to another class, parents, or the rest of your class. Some possibilities follow:

Choral reading with character parts assigned to individuals

Shadow puppet play

Video presentation

Audiocassette with sound effects

Slide show with students drawing original illustrations on blank slide film or on blank overhead transparencies; show the pictures while several students read the book's text

Step 2: Involve your students in the decision-making processes, including the following decisions:

Which presentation mode will be employed?

How will the parts and tasks be divided?

Who will speak which lines?

What props will be needed and how will they be made?

Step 3: For students who complete the assignment early in the week, plan a second assignment, such as independently reading another growing-up story from your literature connections.

Step 4: Perform, and afterward invite students to write a note telling specifically what they were proud of in the performance (for young children, invented spelling or pictures will provide them with the same metacognitive experience).

Adding Metacognitive Steps

Step 1: Once decisions are made and the different tasks assigned, use work sheet 7-2, Intentions and Reflections, at the beginning and end of each work period so that students can engage in the metacognitive process of setting their daily goals and evaluating their progress (see example below; see also technique 7, Intentions and Reflections, on page 277). Students may be working alone or in groups, depending upon earlier decisions.

At the start of each work period, students might write the following:

Today I expect to design the shadow puppets and trace the designs onto the cardboard.

At the end of each work period, students reflect on their progress:

This period I did design most of the puppets, but I have one more to do tomorrow.

All students involved in the project should set clear goals for themselves at the beginning of each work period. If you glance at and star their goal sheets before they begin to work, you will be instantly aware of which students need help. Whenever students are working on a project of their own choosing, whether for a single class period or for many days, the addition of this simple and speedy activity will add greatly to the effectiveness of the project and to a heightened sense of student ownership and responsibility.

Optional Step 2: Take photographs of the performance, and create a class book with students writing explanatory text to accompany the pictures.

Multiple Intelligence Connections

Lesson 7

PARENT INTERVIEW

Prerequisite for Grades 1 through 4

Do lesson 3.

Materials for Each Student

writing paper

pencils

copies of parent note 7-2

Preparation

Duplicate parent note 7-2. Read or reread *Pig Pig Grows Up*.

Procedure

Step 1: Give each student a copy of parent note 7-2. Read it together and be sure that students understand the homework assignment and that they take it home for completion. (If some students are not able to find an adult to help them with the project, provide time early the next day for those students to interview you or another adult in the school so that all can complete the assignment.)

Step 2: The next day, do any or several of the following activities:

- Students retell the adult's growing-up story to a study partner or a study group.

- Grades 1 through 2: After retelling the incident to a partner, students use story paper to draw and write about the incident, using invented spelling.

- Grades 3 through 6: Students write the incident in story form as if it happened to a stranger. Then they read it to a study partner or study group. The story might be critiqued, improved, and added to students' ongoing writing folders for further work at a later date.

- Students write the incident in the first person, as if it happened to them. This activity provides the basis for a good lesson in writing in the first or third person.

If students do any of the writing activities, compile the stories into a class book to read aloud to the class and add it to the class library.

More Challenge

Do the first activity only, then ask students to invent a creative way to present the adult's story to the class. You might suggest some options, such as a comic strip, a poem, a song, a cartoon flip book, a news report, a pantomime, an imagined series of diary entries, or a student-drawn slide or overhead projector show.

Multiple Intelligence Connections

Lesson 8

PLUS AND MINUS

Materials for Each Student

writing paper

pencils

Materials for Whole Class

chalkboard or chart paper for recording class answers

Optional Materials for Grades 5 through 6

work sheet 7-3, Outline for Writing Opinion Papers

Preparation

Make an overhead transparency of work sheet 7-3 and also photo-copy the work sheet for each student. Read or reread *Pig Pig Grows Up*.

Procedure

Step 1: Ask students to give you some reasons Pig Pig may have had for not wanting to grow up. Record them on chart paper or the chalkboard. Invite students to discuss ideas. Then ask them to add any reasons they have for being reluctant to grow up. If your students have been reading their own choice of books about grow-ing up, ask them to think about the growing-up experiences of their main characters.

Step 2: Ask them to tell you some reasons that they are looking forward to growing up. List these in a separate column. If they are reading their own independent books on the topic, ask them to add why growing up was wonderful for their main characters.

Grades 3 and 4

Step 3: Ask students to list on scratch paper at least three reasons why they don't want to grow up and three reasons why they do.

Step 4: Have them read their lists to study partners and place stars by similar answers.

Step 5: Model for students how to write a paragraph about why they don't want to grow up and a paragraph about why they do. Then demonstrate writing a final paragraph telling which desire is stronger and why. Show them how you use the class list of ideas to give justification (see example below).

> *I am not in a hurry to grow up because grown-ups don't seem to have as much time to play as kids do. I also don't want to give up my summer vacation, and I like just hanging out.*

> *I am looking forward to growing up because I don't want anyone telling me what to do and I would like to have a job and make my own money. I would also like to have my own house and family.*

> *I guess I would mostly rather grow up so that I can find out what will happen to me, but I want to take my time.*

Step 6: Ask students to write their own opinion papers modeled after yours but with their own reasons.

Grades 5 and 6

Step 3: Use the format described in technique 11, Writing Opinion Papers, and hand out work sheet 7-3. Tell students that to write an opinion paper they will have to decide whether they would mostly like to grow up or whether they would mostly like to stay young forever. Students can use the two lists they have helped you generate to find reasons to justify their opinions.

Step 4: When all students finish writing their papers, ask them to write on the back of the papers to tell you whether this writing assignment was easy or hard for them, and why (metacognition). When you collect and evaluate the papers, respond to these back-page comments with a written reaction to what was said.

Multiple Intelligence Connections

Lesson 9

IMAGINE AN ENDING TO A GREEK MYTH

Materials

writing paper
pencils

a copy of fact sheet 7-1, the myth of Phaeton and Apollo (page 184)
a world map or globe

Preparation

Read *Pig Pig Grows Up* on a previous day.

Procedure

Step 1: Dim the lights in your classroom and invite students to close their eyes as you read to them. Say, "I will be reading to you a different story about growing up. I will not be reading the entire story, but I will stop before the end so that you can use your imagination to complete the story. When I stop reading, you will have one minute of silence to watch the story unfold. Just imagine that you have a movie screen inside your head. As I read the story, watch what happens on your internal movie screen. Then when I stop reading, continue to watch the screen and see how the story unfolds."

Step 2: Read the story up to the point where Apollo begs Phaeton not to take the chariot of the sun across the sky, and Phaeton must make his decision. Remind students that they have one minute to watch their internal screens to see what Phaeton decides and what happens next.

Step 3: After one minute of silence, say, "Now bring your story to an end and then bring your attention back to the classroom. When I turn the lights up I want you to begin writing. Do not talk, but just start writing about the moment that Phaeton makes his decision and write the part of the story that you saw unfold in your mind's eye. I don't want you to write the entire story, just the ending that you saw on your internal screen. If you didn't see enough during the minute of silence, you can continue to imagine as you write. Ready, begin."

Optional Step 4: After students have written their endings, collect papers and read some of them aloud without naming authors. (Students can acknowledge their work after you have read it.) Or have students work with a partner and read their endings to each other. After reading, both students can sign the bottom of the partner's paper and then move on to a new match. Instruct students to get at least five different signatures.

Step 5: Tell students the "real" ending from the original myth. Phaeton did decide to pull the chariot through the sky. The horses were frightened by the archer, the crab, and the bear. Phaeton could not control them and they came too close to the Earth, scorching and burning every tree in their path and boiling away every river and lake. The place where this happened is still a desert today; it is the Sahara Desert. Finally Zeus struck Phaeton dead with a thunderbolt to stop his destructive ride.

Step 6: Return the students' papers and ask them to write a sentence or two explaining their thoughts or feelings about the mythic ending. Then collect the papers to evaluate or to make written comments reflecting your reaction to their ideas.

Note: This exercise comes from *Picture This: Teaching Reading through Visualization* by Laura Rose. For more information on the importance of teaching students how to create vivid mental images to increase comprehension and reading enjoyment, see technique 9, Visualization, on page 280.

Multiple Intelligence Connections

VENN DIAGRAMS

Materials

work sheet 7-1, Venn Diagram

pencils

Preparation

For background, do lesson 9 and read or reread *Pig Pig Grows Up*. Make a copy of work sheet 7-1 for each student and either draw a similar Venn diagram on a chalkboard or make an overhead transparency of the Venn diagram to use on the overhead projector. Label your diagram with Pig Pig on the left-hand circle and Phaeton on the right.

Procedure

Step 1: Read *Pig Pig Grows Up*.

Step 2: Ask students to tell something about either Pig Pig or Phaeton, such as "he has no father," "he doesn't want to grow up," or "he goes on an adventure." As students raise hands to tell you each element, ask them to help you decide where it should be placed on your Venn diagram and then record it there. Things true only of Pig Pig belong in the left-hand circle, things true only of Phaeton belong in the right-hand circle, and things that are true of both characters belong in the overlapping area (see example below).

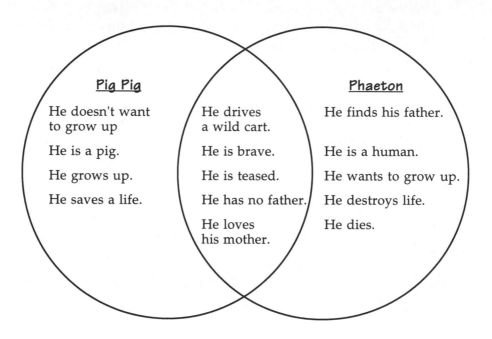

Pig Pig

He doesn't want to grow up

He is a pig.

He grows up.

He saves a life.

He drives a wild cart.

He is brave.

He is teased.

He has no father.

He loves his mother.

Phaeton

He finds his father.

He is a human.

He wants to grow up.

He destroys life.

He dies.

Step 3: After students have added all that they can about these two characters, tell them that they will now compare themselves to whichever character they prefer. Have them use their copies of the Venn diagram and tell them to write their own names above the left-hand circles and either Pig Pig or Phaeton above the right-hand circles. Then challenge them to think of and record ways that they are the same as the story character and ways that they are different from the story character. You may wish to set a minimum of three or four items in each of the three categories and give extra credit for more ideas.

Step 4: Collect papers to evaluate students' understanding of the use of the Venn diagram to compare two characters. You might do this soon with your current read-aloud selection, since all have experience with that story.

More Challenge

Invite students to make another Venn diagram comparing Pig Pig to the main character in their independent reading selections. You might also read aloud Natalie Babbitt's *Tuck Everlasting* so students can make other rich comparisons between its main character and Pig Pig.

Unit

7

MATERIALS

Dear Parent,

As part of our study of children's literature, your child has written and illustrated this book. He or she should be able to read it to you, and I hope you will take the time to listen to it and discuss the words and the pictures. After your child reads this book to you, perhaps you can add it to your home library of children's books. In the future, you might sometimes choose to read this book along with those by more famous authors.

I hope you enjoy and express your pride in your child's work.

Sincerely,

Work Sheet 7-1

Venn Diagram

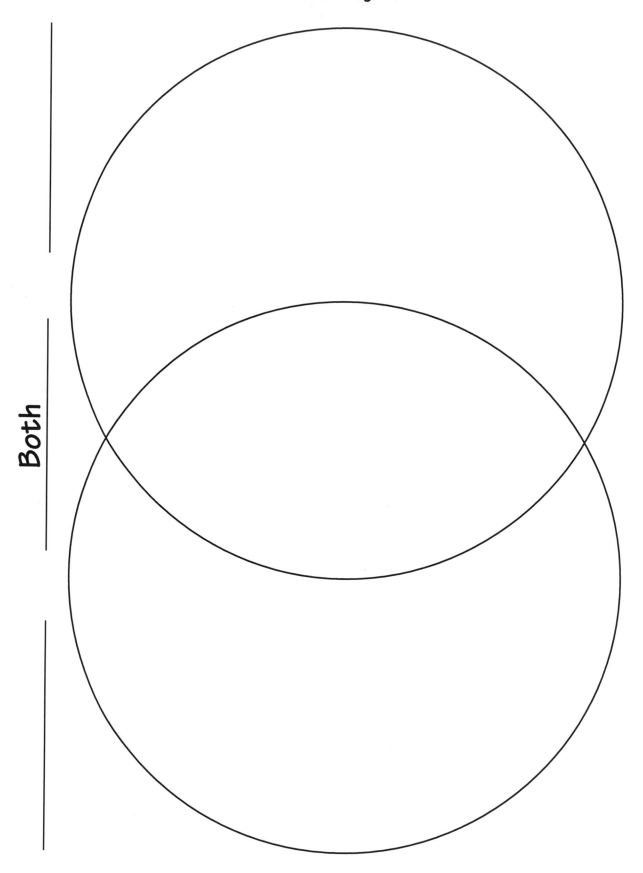

Both

Work Sheet 7-2
Intentions and Reflections
Adding Metacognition to Projects

Date:_____ Today I intend to _____

_____

_____

_____

_____

During this work period, I was able to _____

_____

_____

Tomorrow I hope to

_____

_____

- -

Date:_____ Today I intend to _____

_____

_____

_____

_____

During this work period, I was able to _____

_____

_____

Tomorrow I hope to

_____

_____

- -

Note: For longer projects use additional sheets or have students use a teacher-made journal to make similar daily entries.

Dear Parent,

We are reading books about the pleasures of growing up, and I would like to ask for your help. Your child will be asking you to describe a happy event in your childhood that made you feel that you were definitely growing up. Some parents have told of buying Christmas presents with money they had earned, of going camping or hiking without their parents, of cooking a meal for the family, of getting their first real part-time job, or of learning to ride a bike, ski, or roller skate. Would you be willing to share at least one such experience with your child? Then, in the morning, have your child retell the event to you so that you are sure it is fresh and can be remembered at school. Your child will be sharing this event in an assignment tomorrow.

If you do not wish to participate, your child will be able to interview an adult at school.

Sincerely,

Work Sheet 7-3
Outline for Writing Opinion Papers

1st paragraph: State your opinion and three reasons to justify it.

_____

_____

_____

_____

_____

2nd paragraph: Expand on your first reason.

_____

_____

_____

_____

_____

3rd paragraph: Expand on your second reason.

_____

_____

_____

_____

_____

4th paragraph: Expand on your third reason.

_____

_____

_____

_____

_____

5th paragraph: Restate your opinion and close.

_____

_____

_____

_____

_____

Fact Sheet 7-1

The Myth of Phaeton and Apollo

Long ago and far away in a small village in ancient Greece, a handsome young boy named Phaeton lived with his mother, whom he loved and honored.

But as much as he loved his mother, he could not help but miss having a father. His friends and schoolmates often teased him. His mother told him that his father had loved her very much and would have loved him too, if only he could, but his father was not a mortal. He was Apollo, one of the gods, and gods were not allowed to live with mortals, even if they fell in love. The gods must live together on Mount Olympus where they could watch over the human race.

Apollo had a particularly important job. He pulled the sun across the sky every day in a golden chariot drawn by seven immortal horses. His work brought light to the world, allowing the crops to grow and the earth to flourish. He could not possibly leave that vital work to come and live in a small house in an insignificant village.

When Phaeton's friends taunted him about his missing father, he told them his mother's story, but they laughed. They did not believe that Phaeton was the son of a god. They all knew that Apollo was the god who pulled the fiery sun's chariot across the skies. Phaeton could not possibly be the son of the powerful god who could do that. Phaeton was angry and embarrassed at the disbelief of his friends, so one day he decided to do something that would prove to them that he truly was the son of Apollo.

For several days he thought and wondered about how to prove that Apollo was his father. Finally, he thought of a plan. He decided to visit his father and ask to drive the sun's chariot across the sky. If his friends saw him driving the chariot that pulled the sun, they would know the truth of his words.

Phaeton traveled far and long, down dusty roads, past homes both poor and rich. After much walking, his path brought him to the foot of Mount Olympus, the home of the gods. It stretched high above his young head.

The way up the mountain to the palace of the sun is steep and awesome, but Phaeton was strong and determined to succeed and finally the palace loomed before him. As he approached, huge silver doors opened to reveal an immense hall. The light from within was almost more than he could bear. It shone from the throne at the end of the hall, a throne made of gold encrusted with diamonds and shimmering almost as brightly as the sun itself. Seated on this magnificent throne was Apollo himself. He was robed in deepest purple and crowned with rubies and amethysts.

Apollo instantly recognized Phaeton as his son and made him welcome. He asked the young man why he came on this long, hard journey. Phaeton explained the trouble that he had with his friends, and told his father that he had a favor to ask. Out of his deep love for his son, Apollo granted him any wish that he might have. Phaeton asked to drive the sun chariot across the sky.

Imagine this moment in your mind's eye.

Apollo was thunderstruck. He begged Phaeton to reconsider, to ask him for anything but that. Driving the sun's chariot was beyond the power of a mere mortal. The horses were almost too much for even the mighty Apollo to control. And if the chariot were to get out of control, it would go too low and scorch the earth, setting homes and fields afire. If it went too high, it would burn the heavens and the homes of the gods, and the earth would be left to freeze.

Even if Phaeton could keep the chariot on its course, there were terrible monsters that must be avoided: the wild bull, the archer, the lion, the scorpion, and the crab. It was dangerous beyond belief.

But there was nothing else Phaeton wanted as much as this one favor. His friends would know beyond a doubt that he was the child of Apollo if he could drive the sun's chariot through the skies.

Once more Apollo begged his son to change his mind. He said that if Phaeton insisted, he must keep his promise, but he would grant any other wish if Phaeton would just release him from his pledge. Phaeton knew that his father was right about the dangers of the journey, but the sky beckoned, and he remembered the taunts of his friends. What will he decide?

Stop and allow one minute of silence for students to imagine.

Note: This version of the myth is adapted from *Picture This: Teaching Reading through Visualization* by Laura Rose.

Developing Intelligences through Literature © 1996 Zephyr Press, Tucson, AZ

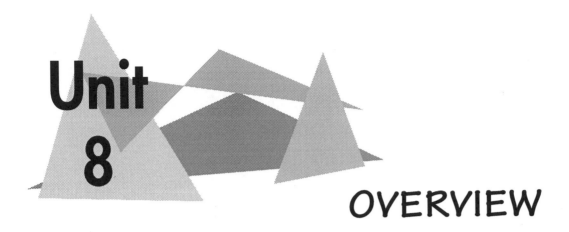

Unit 8

OVERVIEW

Central Literature Selection:
Save Queen of Sheba
by Louise Moeri

Unit Focus:
Making Difficult Decisions
Grades: 4–5

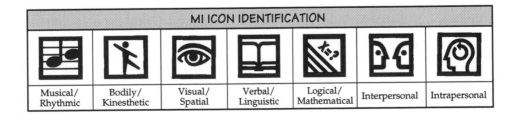

THINKING SKILLS SYMBOLS IDENTIFICATION				
Personal Connection	Creation	Mastery	Reasoning	Metacognition

MI ICON IDENTIFICATION						
Musical/ Rhythmic	Bodily/ Kinesthetic	Visual/ Spatial	Verbal/ Linguistic	Logical/ Mathematical	Interpersonal	Intrapersonal

Lesson 1: **Response Journals** (Grades 4–5; five minutes or more each day)

As the chapters are read, students write thoughtful responses in a teacher-made book in which the teacher makes personal responses to the students' comments.

Lesson 2: **Free Reading Choices** (Grades 4–5; thirty minutes each day)

For independent reading students select a book from literature connections or any other book about making decisions and read it independently. Brief oral reports and an optional book report are made to the class periodically.

Lesson 3: **Living on a Wagon** (Grades 4–5; one class period)

Students figure out a way to draw the outlines of life-size wagons and oxen so that they can get a sense of the size of the travelers' homes.

Lesson 4: **What's in a Name?** (Grades 4–5; homework and two class periods)

After the class learns how King David and Queen of Sheba's parents decided on their names, students explore the meanings and origins of their own names.

Lesson 5: **Why "Westward, Ho!"?** (Grades 4–5; one class period)

Students engage in the double-entry format of guesses and facts to find out about why people faced all the dangers of the westward movement.

Lesson 6: **Westward Ho! Posters** (Grades 4–5; three or more art periods)

After learning why people moved west in Lesson 5, student partners make posters to convince easterners to decide to move west.

Lesson 7: **Pioneer Music and Dance** (Grades 4–5; one or more class periods)

Students enjoy and participate in pioneer music and dance.

Lesson 8: **Writing a Camp Song** (Grades 4–5; two or more class periods)

Using the tune of the pioneer song "Oleanna," students help to write their own verses following the tradition of the pioneers.

Lesson 9: **Decisions and Consequences** (Grades 4–5; a few minutes each day)

Students apply their study of decisions to themselves and start daily goal-setting and reflection to increase their senses of personal responsibility.

Lesson 10: **Best Decisions** (Grades 4–5; homework and one class period)

Students reflect on some good decisions that they have made in their lives and explore the consequences.

Synopsis of *Save Queen of Sheba*

Save Queen of Sheba is a gripping story of King David, a 12-year-old boy who survives the massacre of his wagon train only to find that he is now responsible for saving his stubborn and helpless little sister, Queen of Sheba. The story takes them through the wild country where King David is faced with a series of decisions that will mean the difference between life or death for them both.

Explanation of Unit Focus: Making Difficult Decisions

This unit asks students to think about the importance of making good decisions. They consider the decisions that King David, like all the other pioneers of the westward movement, had to make for himself and his sister. Students explore reasons for decisions as well as consequences of decisions.

Cross-Curricular Connections

You might link this lesson to your anti-drug or other health-related units. Such units usually have materials that discuss decision-making because decisions are a central part of helping children say "no" to things that will harm them and say "yes" to healthy choices. Also link to a direction-finding unit in science or geography.

Response Journals

The response journal is a project that continues regularly during the reading of the book, and it can serve to organize your unit. If you do not choose to do the journals, you can still do any of the other lessons and pick a few of the suggested response journal activities without doing the whole project.

To Start the Unit

Look at the suggested lessons and select those that are appropriate for your class. Hand out the teacher-made response journals (see technique 10, Response Journals, on page 281) and read the first two chapters aloud to your class. If you have a class set, assign the first two chapters; provide help for students who cannot read the book independently so they can keep up with the rest of the class. If you do not wish to do response journals, read *Save Queen of Sheba* aloud to your students, stopping after each appropriate chapter to engage in the lessons you select.

Literature Connections

Following is a list of books on the unit's focus for your students to read independently during the unit and even after you have finished the unit. If each student is reading a different book, discussions and activities regarding the unit's focus will be far richer than if everyone reads the same selection. See technique 1, Free Reading with Literature Connections, for suggestions.

Books

Anderson, Margaret. 1978. *Searching for Shona*. Knopf.

Avi. 1986. *Wolf Rider*. Bradbury.

Babbitt, Natalie. 1975. *Tuck Everlasting*. Farrar, Straus and Giroux.

Bauer, Marion Dane. 1986. *On My Honor*. Clarion.

Bawden, Nina. 1982. *Squib*. Lothrop.

Bishop, Claire Huchet. 1952. *Twenty and Ten*. Viking.

Brandel, Marc. 1974. *Mine of Lost Days*. Lippincott.

Bulla, Clyde Robert. 1981. *Lion to Guard Us*. Harper.

Byars, Betsy. 1985. *Cracker Johnson*. Viking.

Cleaver, Vera, and Bill Cleaver. 1969. *Where the Lilies Bloom*. Lippincott.

Collier, James. 1974. *My Brother Sam Is Dead*. Four Winds.

Conrad, Pam. 1989. *My Daniel*. Harper.

Davies, Andrew. 1980. *Conrad's War*. Crown.

Fine, Anne. 1983. *The Granny Project*. Farrar, Straus and Giroux.

Forbes, Esther. 1943. *Johnny Tremain*. Houghton Mifflin.

George, Jean C. 1959. *My Side of the Mountain*. Dutton.

Hahn, Mary Downing. 1983. *Daphne's Book*. Houghton Mifflin.

Holland, Isabelle. 1978. *Dinah and the Far Green Kingdom*. Lippincott.

Hughes, Dean. 1982. *Honestly, Myron*. Atheneum.

Hurmence, Belinda. 1982. *Girl Called Boy*. Houghton Mifflin.

Lamour, Louis. 1968. *Down the Long Hills*. Bantam.

Mathis, Sharon Bell. 1986. *The Hundred Penny Box*. Puffin Books.

Mazer, Harry. 1986. *Cave under the City*. Crowell.

Moeri, Louise. 1984. *Downwind*. Dutton.

O'Dell, Scott. 1960. *Island of the Blue Dolphins*. Houghton Mifflin.

Paulsen, Gary. 1988. *Voyage of the Frog*. Orchard.

Polese, Carolyn. 1978. *Something about a Mermaid*. Dutton.

Rawls, Wilson. 1976. *Summer of the Monkeys*. Doubleday.

Reiss, Johanna. 1972. *Upstairs Room*. Crowell.

Robinson, Barbara. 1972. *Best Christmas Pageant Ever*. Harper.

Ruckman, Ivy. 1988. *No Way Out*. Crowell.

Schlee, Ann. 1976. *Ask Me No Questions*. Holt.

Taylor, Mildred. 1987. *The Friendship*. Dial.

Taylor, Theodore. 1969. *The Cay*. Doubleday.

Winthrop, Elizabeth. 1985. *Castle in the Attic*. Harper.

RESPONSE JOURNALS

Materials

teacher-made writing books

pencils

Preparation

Make response journals for each student (see technique 5, Teacher-Made Books, on page 273). If you are unused to response journals be sure to refer to technique 10, Response Journals, page 281 for an overview of how to ensure the most student involvement.

Designed to stimulate students' thoughtful interaction with the story, this activity will continue all during the reading of *Save Queen of Sheba*. On these pages you will find specific activities to do with the response journals after certain story chapters. If other, better questions or activities occur to you, do not hesitate to substitute them for mine. Always be aware, however, of students' need for privacy and right to choose whether or not to share life events with you.

Procedure

Step 1: After reading chapters 1 and 2, brainstorm with your students and write on the board a list of decisions that King David has made so far. Ask students why they think he made each of the decisions.

Step 2: Ask students to tell you in their journals how they felt about King David's decisions.

Step 3: After reading chapter 3, ask students to make their own lists of King David's decisions in today's reading.

Step 4: Have them show their lists to partners and add to their lists any decisions with which they agree from their partners' lists.

Step 5: Have students raise hands to share so you can write the decisions in one complete list on a chart or on the board.

Step 6: Ask students to respond in journals to the following and give at least one reason for each of their responses:

Which of King David's decisions did you applaud?

Which are you not too sure of?

Step 7: Read chapter 4. Do not have students make a response journal entry; you might do lesson 3.

Step 8: After reading chapter 5, have students list decisions as they did after chapter 3, first individually, then with partners, then generate a whole-class list.

Step 9: Ask students to respond in journals to the following:

> *Which was the most important decision King David made in this chapter?*
>
> *Why do you think he decided to do it?*
>
> *Why was it so important?*

Optional Step 10: Display the results of this vote as a graph.

Step 11: After reading chapter 6, do lesson 4.

Step 12: After reading chapters 7 and 8, ask students to list decisions that children make every day that can be a matter of life and death. Have them share their responses with the class and create a class list. You could also do lesson 5 and begin lesson 6, which deal with reasons people were moving west.

Step 13: After reading chapter 9, brainstorm and discuss King David's decisions in today's reading.

Step 14: Ask students to write why they think King David didn't kill the snake; discuss the students' ideas.

Step 15: Ask students to write what King David found on the trail that helped him understand why the Indians had attacked his wagon. (It was the bones of the slaughtered bison). Discuss King David's understanding and his apparent lack of bitterness toward the Indians at this point in the story. This discussion should help them understand why King David decides not to shoot an Indian boy later.

Step 16: After reading chapters 10 and 11, do not have students write in their response journals. Do lesson 7.

Step 17: After reading chapters 12 and 13, ask students to draw a line down the center of a journal page. Label one column "continue on" and label the other "keep searching."

Step 18: Ask students to work with partners to find reasons that King David should decide to make each of these choices.

Step 19: With the whole class, discuss the students' ideas. You could make a whole-class list of reasons for each choice.

Step 20: Ask each student to write what he or she thinks King David should do and why. After this writing and discussion, students' answers should be much more thoughtful and rich than before.

Step 21: After reading chapters 14 through 16, discuss King David's decision not to shoot the Indian boy. Talk about how a good decision is made. Ask students to help you list King David's probable reasons for not shooting the boy.

Step 22: Ask students to write about this incident in their journals, telling their thoughts and feelings.

Step 23: After reading chapter 17, ask students why they think King David decided to try to save Queen of Sheba. After you discuss and list each suggestion, ask students to write an answer to each of the following:

> *Which of these reasons do you think made King David go back for Queen of Sheba once more?*

> *What do you think you would have done? Why?*

Multiple Intelligence Connections

Lesson 2

FREE READING CHOICES

Materials

books from literature connections and any other books you can gather that deal with making important decisions

Preparation

Gather as many books as you can find about making important decisions (see Literature Connections, page 190, for suggestions).

Procedure

Have students read freely in self-selected books for an extended period each day. Also have them engage in some form of reporting their reading to the class, such as that described in the intermediate grades section of technique 1, Free Reading with Literature Connections, on page 267.

Multiple Intelligence Connections

Lesson 3

LIVING ON A WAGON

Materials

chalk

rulers

whatever else students ask for to help them draw the wagons accurately

Preparation

Read at least through chapter 4 of *Save Queen of Sheba*.

Procedure

Step 1: Organize students into groups of three or four and give each group a ruler and the dimensions of a typical wagon. The Prairie Schooner, which was the most common wagon for pioneer families to use, usually measured about four feet by twelve feet.

Step 2: Take students outside and challenge them to find a way to draw the wagon outline on the blacktop or concrete. Tell them that you want the lines drawn straight and that the corners should form right angles.

Step 3: Coach the groups as they work, asking them about their processes to be sure that all lines are the correct length and will meet at all four corners in right angles.

Step 4: Have the groups get into their wagons and sit down to feel the size of their home on wheels. If you have been learning a pioneer song, such as "Oh, Susannah" or "Sweet Betsy from Pike," the students might enjoy singing it now.

Optional Step 5: Back in the classroom, discuss the experience and ask students to write in their response journals to tell you what they think and feel about what they have just learned about the size of the wagons.

More Challenge

Ask students to write down and turn in what they did and how they figured out how to do it, including the math that they used. They can include a diagram (metacognition).

Multiple Intelligence Connections

Lesson 4

WHAT'S IN A NAME?

Materials

books that explain the meaning of first names (many dictionaries have such a section at the back)

optional: a Bible or an abbreviated version of the story of King David and the story of the Queen of Sheba

Preparation

Gather books that list names and their meanings. Read *Save Queen of Sheba* through chapter 6, in which the children's names are explained.

Procedure

Step 1: Discuss the explanation in chapter 6 of how the children got their names. Tell students that the author of this book actually had ancestors with these names. Her ancestors lived during the time of the westward movement.

Optional Step 2: Show or read to students the stories of the biblical King David and Queen of Sheba as a cultural reference.

Step 3: Tell students to ask their parents how they chose their children's names. Students can write their findings along with a personal reaction to their parents' stories.

Step 4: Next day, let students find the meaning of their own names in the books you supply.

Step 5: Either on a sheet of paper or in the response journals if you are using them, ask students to write the answers to the following questions:

> *How did you get your first name? (If you don't know, make up a great story)*
>
> *What does your first name mean?*
>
> *What does your middle name mean?*
>
> *If you could choose a different name, what would it be? Choose a new first and a new middle name. (Look through the name books for ideas.)*

More Challenge

Students interview relatives to find out how they got their names and report on their research in the format of a family tree with explanations.

Multiple Intelligence Connections

Lesson 5

WHY "WESTWARD, HO!"?

Materials for Each Student

lined paper

pencils

Material for the teacher

fact sheet 8-1, Settlement of California and Oregon

Preparation

Make a copy of fact sheet 8-1 for each student. Read *Save Queen of Sheba* at least through chapter 4.

Procedure

Step 1: Tell students to fold their papers in half vertically, open them, and draw a line down the center of the page. Then have them write the numbers from 1 to 10 along the left-hand edge.

Step 2: Ask students the ten questions from the bottom of fact sheet 8-1, and have them record their guesses in the first column. Assure the class that their answers will not be graded, but you do want their best guesses. Tell them that they are guaranteed of an "A" on this lesson if their answers are correct after you read the fact sheet to them and if they correct any errors.

Step 3: Now read fact sheet 8-1 aloud, with students raising their hands every time one of the ten questions is answered. If they guessed correctly, they can mark their correct guess with a C. If they guessed incorrectly, they should draw a line through the guess and put the correct answer in the right-hand column across from the guess (see example below). Students tend to be very motivated to find out whether their guesses are correct. For some questions, there can be more than one correct answer, and these questions should lead to interesting discussion.

Guesses	Confirmed
1. ~~diamonds~~	fur, and hides
2. yes C	
3. ~~No~~	yes, if you lived on it and built a house
4. ~~a gun and bullets~~	a rifle and an ax
5. ~~the railroad~~	and the U.S. Government

Step 4: When students have written the correct response to all ten questions, collect their papers. Remind students that they are guaranteed an "A" on this lesson if they have all of the answers finally correct. There is no such thing as cheating on this assignment, because the value of the lesson lies in the process of guessing, getting interested, and then finding out the facts.

Multiple Intelligence Connections

Lesson 6

WESTWARD, HO! POSTERS

Materials

art materials of your choice to make Westward, Ho! posters

work sheet 8-1, Intentions and Reflections

Preparation

Read *Save Queen of Sheba* at least through chapter 4 and do lesson 5. Make a copy of work sheet 8-1 for each student.

Procedure

Step 1: From your discussion during lesson 5, remind the class of the reasons that people decided to move west in those times.

Step 2: Challenge students to create posters that would have enticed people to move from the east to Oregon or California. Require both text and illustrations. Have students work alone, in pairs, or in cooperative learning groups.

Step 3: You may wish to decide on the media involved, or if students have had a variety of art experiences, you could let them decide. In this case, first ask the class to help you list possibilities, such as the following:

> *water color*
>
> *crayon*
>
> *cut paper*
>
> *pen and ink*
>
> *torn paper*
>
> *tissue paper layers or rosettes*
>
> *computer-generated art*
>
> *potato prints*
>
> *paint with strips of oil-based clay*
>
> *felt-tip pen*
>
> *stamp art*

Step 4: When the posters are completed, ask each student to write three good things about their posters and turn them into you with the posters to influence your evaluation.

Adding Metacognition

Step 1: Give students each a copy of work sheet 8-1 so they can keep track of their progress over the next few class periods as they work on this project. You may want to review technique 7, Intentions and Reflections, on page 277.

Step 2: Require students to make a working sketch and a list of materials for you to check and approve before they start work. They can make their lists on the back of work sheet 8-1. Whenever students are working on a project of their own choosing, whether for a single class period or for many days, the addition of this simple and speedy work sheet will add greatly to the effectiveness of the project and to a heightened sense of student ownership and responsibility.

Multiple Intelligence Connections

PIONEER MUSIC AND DANCE

Materials

songs and recordings of dances from pioneer times

Preparation

Gather songs and instructions for dances from pioneer times. Try to find a square dance caller, a fiddler, or a cowboy musician to visit your class to perform and teach students songs and dances.

Procedure

Step 1: Teach your students songs and dances from pioneer times. As part of these lessons, you might invite someone qualified to your class to help you.

Step 2: Ask students to write down then discuss the following questions with a partner or with the whole class.

Why do you think that so many pioneers made the choice to include singing and dancing in their lives?

What kinds of music do you choose to include in your life?

What does the choice of music add to your own life?

More Challenge

End the discussion with having students write opinion papers on one of the following topics: "Why Music Was Important to Pioneers" or "Why Music Is Important to Me" (see technique 11, Writing Opinion Papers, page 282, for suggestions).

Multiple Intelligence Connections

Lesson 8

WRITING A CAMP SONG

Materials

the words and music to "Cali-, California" on page 208

Preparation

Read at least half of *Save Queen of Sheba*. Learn the tune to "Cali-, California."

Procedure

Step 1: Talk to students about the lack of entertainment on the trail in the evenings. Sitting around the campfire, folks would often sing to relieve their boredom and lift their spirits. Someone might have a banjo or a fiddle or a harmonica. But after a while, they would get tired of the same old song, and so they would begin to make up new verses.

Step 2: Tell your students that you are going to teach them the tune of a real pioneer song, and they are going to make up some verses.

Step 3: Teach them one verse and the chorus, then present one of the partial verses on the song sheet. Sing it or write it on the board.

Or make an overhead transparency out of the song sheet and fill it in as students invent verses.

Step 4: To help students think of the additional lines to each verse, brainstorm words that rhyme with the last word of the first line. Then work together, calling out ideas, changing and playing with them, until the right idea strikes and you reach consensus. These songs are supposed to cheer people up, so keep an eye out for humor. The pioneers are also probably sick and tired of the trail, the food, the dust, the dangers, so the verses might reflect their difficulties and their wishes.

Step 5: After you have written as many verses as you want to write, sing them all.

Optional Step 6: Have students practice excellent handwriting by copying the verses they have written. They will have practiced a needed skill while making a copy that they would like to keep.

Optional Step 7: Find someone who plays the fiddle, guitar, banjo, or harmonica and ask that person to accompany the class as they sing the song they wrote.

More Challenge

Students write a verse or two of their own, without using your beginning lines. Students may also use this tune to write a song about an interest of theirs, such as baseball, soap operas, or life at school.

Multiple Intelligence Connections

Lesson 9

DECISIONS AND CONSEQUENCES

Materials

pencils

teacher-made books

Preparation

Make a book with eight sheets of lined paper for each student (see technique 5, Teacher-Made Books, on page 273). This lesson is meant to help students develop a sense of responsibility and personal power. It is particularly helpful to students who are always blaming other people for what they see as their own bad luck. Through setting a goal each day and reflecting on the success of that goal, students begin to recognize how they can have considerable charge over how their day goes. Read some of *Save Queen of Sheba* and do at least one other lesson about decisions.

Procedure

Step 1: At the start of the school day, distribute teacher-made books. Ask students to write a simple, specific goal for the day, something that they think will make part of their day go well (see example below).

Acceptable	Too Much
I will have my pencil sharp before math.	I will pay attention all day.
I will be in class on time after lunch.	I will be good.
I will not talk to Sue at silent reading.	I won't get mad.
I will not cut in the lunch line.	I'll do great work.
I will get my book out quickly at reading time.	I'll be nice at recess.
I will use good handwriting today.	My papers will all be perfect.
I will check each paper for spelling errors.	I won't make any mistakes.

Step 2: At the end of the day, have students tell whether they accomplished their goals, and what the result was (see example below).

I was on time from lunch and nothing happened but I got my work done.

I wasn't on time from lunch and I had to sit 10 minutes at p.e.

If you do this activity daily, your students may begin to realize that they often set themselves up for difficulty. They may perhaps begin to realize that they can set themselves up for success instead. Over the course of time, this exercise can make a positive difference in the tone of your classroom and success level of your students. (For more information about this approach, read Eva Fugitt, *He Hit Me Back First*, Jalmar Press, 1982.)

Multiple Intelligence Connections

BEST DECISIONS

Materials

paper

pencils

Preparation

Do this lesson after your class has read at least half of *Save Queen of Sheba*.

Procedure

Step 1: Have students spend time recalling and listing good decisions that they have made in their lives. They can ask parents for help. Give students some hints about the kind of decisions that you would like them to list (see list below).

> *to study a musical instrument*
>
> *to join a team or a club*
>
> *to do someone a favor*
>
> *to do something nice for someone*
>
> *to volunteer for a job or responsibility*
>
> *to learn how to do something, like ride a bike, sew, cook*
>
> *to start a collection*
>
> *to solve a problem, such as being lost*
>
> *to make up with someone*
>
> *to break a bad habit*

Step 2: The next day at school, have students share their lists with partners and add more items to the lists as they think of more decisions of which they are proud.

Step 3: Tell students that they are going to write about one of the good decisions their partners had made. Write the following questions on the board:

Which decision do you want me to write about?

What made you come to that decision?

Why was it a good decision?

Step 4: Ask a student volunteer to let you use one of her or his decisions to write a sample paper in front of the class. Model, asking that student the three questions and writing about this decision.

Step 5: Have students interview each other and write their papers about the decisions they find out about in the interviews.

Unit
8

MATERIALS

Fact Sheet 8-1

Settlement of California and Oregon

Every person who decided to travel to Oregon or California on the wagon trains had his and her own special reason for going. We can never know why many chose to pack up their families and belongings and leave a safe home, friends, and family for the hunger, thirst, and danger of the wagon train. But a study of history can help us make some guesses.

The first people to move west were mostly single men. Hunters and trappers came west for the money that they could get from the fur and hides of beaver, buffalo, bear, fox, and seal. Others moved west because they loved to travel freely from town to town with no one to call boss.

Some of the earliest travelers were hired by governments to explore the lands that lay beyond the Mississippi River.

Lewis and Clark traveled overland all the way to the Pacific Ocean. Zebulon Pike went to the Rocky Mountains where a mountain, Pike's Peak in Colorado, is named after him. People all along the east coast heard the explorers' reports about the beauty of the western lands and began to wonder if life wasn't better out west.

About this time the United States government and the men who owned the railroads began to encourage more people to move west. The government wanted to be able to expand its size by populating more territories and turning them into states. The railroad wanted to stretch all the way across the country, and it needed many towns along the way to pay for its services.

The railroad advertised with great enthusiasm and more than a little exaggeration, making California and Oregon sound like paradise on earth. The government made the price of land cheaper and cheaper, until under the Prairie Homestead Act of 1862, a person could own 40 acres out west with just a willingness to settle and improve the land. More and more families became interested. Then the people who had already moved west wanted the company of the people they had left behind, so they wrote letters telling their friends and relatives how wonderful life in the west was. Perhaps they exaggerated just a bit so that they could have good neighbors, but we will never know.

Back in the eastern states, it was getting crowded. New arrivals from countries such as Scotland, England, Germany, Wales, and Scandinavia were finding that every bit of the east coast was already owned by someone. The open west drew these immigrants like a magnet. Some religious groups, such as the Mormons, experienced prejudice and open hostility; they wanted to move west to gain religious freedom.

It took from six to eight months to go by sea, but many a ship went down to a watery grave rounding the tip of South America. Most people chose to go by wagon trains that were pulled by horses, oxen, or cattle.

Developing Intelligences through Literature © 1996 Zephyr Press, Tucson, AZ

It cost about $600.00 to outfit a wagon and fully loaded it weighed about 1,500 to 2,000 pounds. The two items no pioneer could do without were an axe and a rifle. Men alone on horseback and families in covered wagons all carried those two essentials for hunting and self-protection, and for chopping wood and for building homes in the new land.

The trail was long and hard. Water was scarce, and sickness often struck the travelers, killing many. Yet, despite the hardships of the trail, many thousands decided to go. These people were looking for a new chance, a new hope, better farmland, more freedom. They would settle down to build the farms and the towns, the churches and the schools, expanding the nation from shore to shore.

1. Before gold was discovered, what other riches did people come west to find?

2. Did anyone move west for freedom of religion?

3. Was land ever completely free?

4. Besides food, what two items did every family carry if they were going west by wagon or horseback?

5. What kinds of animals pulled the wagons?

6. Who went west first, mostly families or mostly lone hunters and trappers?

7. Who discovered Pike's Peak?

8. Did more people move west by sea around South America or by wagon train?

9. Did the U.S. government like the idea of many families moving out west?

10. Was the wagon train trip easy and safe or difficult and dangerous?

Song

Cali-, California

(sung to the tune of Oleanna, new words by Laura Rose)

Well, I wish I was in California, that is where I'd rather be,

Than ridin' on this wagon train, I know you folks will all agree.

Cali- Californ - i - a, Cali- Californ - i - a, Gotta get to, gotta get to, get to Cali- forn - i - a!

1. Ridin' on this wagon train—both my shoes are plumb wore out,
   If I wasn't half way there _____

2. When I ride behind the train, I'm filled with dust from head to toe,
   But if I ride on up ahead _____

3. When we left home, we were headed for a place called paradise,
   But now we think we'd settle for _____

4. When it's supper time, we gather with our tongues all hanging out,
   But the cookie smiles and tells us _____

5. We've been tired and we've been hungry—been so cold our fingers froze,
   But we'll never quit because _____

Possible Answers (Teacher's Cheat Sheet)

1. I'd turn this wagon round about!
2. I'm sure I won't know where to go!
3. a place that's got some beans and rice!
4. no more food, we'll do without!
5. this is the life that we have chose.

Developing Intelligences through Literature © 1996 Zephyr Press, Tucson, AZ

Work Sheet 8-1
Intentions and Reflections
Adding Metacognition to Projects

Date:_____ Today I intend to _____

_____

_____

_____

_____

During this work period, I was able to _____

_____

_____

Tomorrow I hope to

_____

_____

- -

Date:_____ Today I intend to _____

_____

_____

_____

_____

During this work period, I was able to _____

_____

_____

Tomorrow I hope to

_____

_____

- -

Note: For longer projects use additional sheets or have students use a teacher-made journal to make similar daily entries.

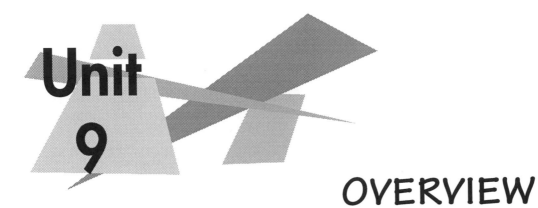

Unit 9

OVERVIEW

Central Literature Selection:
Abel's Island
by William Steig

Unit Focus:
Heroic Fantasy Adventures
Grades: 5–6

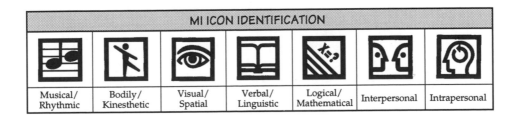

THINKING SKILLS SYMBOLS IDENTIFICATION				
Personal Connection	Creation	Mastery	Reasoning	Metacognition

MI ICON IDENTIFICATION						
Musical/ Rhythmic	Bodily/ Kinesthetic	Visual/ Spatial	Verbal/ Linguistic	Logical/ Mathematical	Interpersonal	Intrapersonal

Lesson 1:   **Response Journals** (Grades 5–6; five minutes or more each day)

As the chapters are read, students make thoughtful responses in a teacher-made book; teacher makes personal responses in conversational style.

Lesson 2:   **Free Reading Choices** (Grades 5–6; twenty to thirty minutes each day)

Students read other books that focus on the unit's theme.

Lesson 3:   **A Real Island Home** (Grades 5–6; five minutes each chapter)

Students create a real island and add elements to it after each chapter is read. This activity really makes the story come alive.

Lesson 4:   **Abel's Boat** (Grades 5–6; one or two class periods)

Students draw or design and test a model of Abel's Boat.

Lesson 5:   **Mouse House** (Grades 5–6; several art periods)

Students create Abel's city home and its elegant mouse furniture by using their imaginations, a few boxes, and an assortment of art materials.

Lesson 6:   **Critical Attributes of Plants** (Grades 5–6; one class period)

Students classify plants according to categories set up by the teacher.

Lesson 7:   **Edible Plant Research** (Grades 5–6; two or more class periods)

By doing research on edible plants and then writing a story segment using that information, students learn the work that authors do before writing.

Lesson 8:   **The Hero's Journey** (Grades 5–6; two or more class periods)

Students learn the six elements in most hero's journeys. They analyze the familiar *Wizard of Oz* to learn the six steps and then apply what they have learned to Abel's Island.

Lesson 9:   **More Heroes' Journeys** (Grades 5–6; one or more class periods)

Students analyze their independent-reading selections according to the elements of the hero's journey and then do an oral presentation or sell the book to the class.

Lesson 10:   **Compare with *Beauty and the Beast*** (Grades 5–6; two or more class periods)

Students view or read *Beauty and the Beast* and then compare it with *Abel's Island* to see how the elements of the hero's journey are found in both.

Lesson 11:   **Writing Your Own Hero's Journey** (Grades 5–6; two class periods)

Students use creative visualization and the six steps of the typical hero's journey to write their own fantasy adventures. They may also edit, publish, illustrate, and share these stories.

Lesson 12: **Personification** (Grades 5–6)

Students learn about the literary device of personification, often used in tales of heroic journeys.

Lesson 13: **Heroic Music** (Grades 5–6)

Students visualize heroic journeys while listening to music, then draw their images.

Synopsis of *Abel's Island*

Abel's Island is a gentle, absorbing fantasy about a fastidious mouse with inherited wealth and a perfect marriage who is stranded on an island in a hurricane. Unsuccessful in his ingenious attempts to escape the island, he longs for the life and the love he has left, yet he learns to delve into and enjoy life in the wild. Because the vocabulary and writing style are very sophisticated, this book is an excellent read-aloud with opportunities to discuss the meaning of unusual words.

Explanation of Unit Focus: Heroic Fantasy Adventures

Students are asked to think about this particular genre of fiction. Students will explore the six elements often found in heroic journeys, and will read and compare at least one other book of this genre. The unit will culminate with students writing a heroic journey of their own and rewriting Abel's story from his wife's viewpoint.

Cross-Curricular Connections

If you involve students in the lessons in which they create their own stories, you can have them do research on the geographical areas in which their stories are set. They may also do research on any science that is a part of their stories. You can also work on writing skills such as personification, metaphor, and simile as the students are polishing their stories.

Use of the Lessons That Follow

These lessons are arranged in an approximate order along with any work sheets or other pages that might be needed. I do not intend that you use all of the lessons, but do select those lessons that complement each other. For example, lesson 1 can only be done fully if you also do lesson 2.

Response Journals

The response journal is a project that continues regularly during the reading of the book, and it can serve to organize your unit. If you do not choose to do the journals, you can still do any of the other lessons, and you can pick some of the suggested response journal activities without doing them all.

To Start the Unit

Look at the suggested lessons and select those that are appropriate for your class. If you are doing lesson 1, hand out the teacher-made books (see technique 5, Teacher-Made Books, page 273). Then read the first chapter aloud to your class. If you have a class set of the books, assign the first chapter, being sure that students who cannot read it on their own are helped in some way to keep up with the rest of the class. If you do not wish to do response journals, read aloud *Abel's Island* to your students, stopping after each appropriate chapter to engage in the lessons you select.

You may also ask each student to select a book from the literature connections list to read individually while you are reading *Abel's Island,* although this step is not critical. Students will report on these books in lesson 9.

Literature Connections

Following is a list of books on the unit's focus for your students to read independently during the unit and even after you have finished the unit. If each student is reading a different book, discussions and activities regarding the unit's focus will be far richer than if everyone reads the same selection. See technique 1, Free Reading with Literature Connections, for suggestions.

Alexander, Lloyd. 1964. *Book of Three.* *Holt.

Babbitt, Natalie. 1969. *Search for Delicious.* Farrar, Straus and Giroux.

Baum, L. Frank. 1979. *The Wizard of Oz.* *Ballantine.

Chant, Joy. 1977. *Red Moon and Black Mountain.* *Unwin.

Chetwin, Grace. 1986. *Gom on Windy Mountain.* *Lothrop.

Cooper, Susan. 1965. *Over Sea, Under Stone.**Macmillan.

————. 1983. *Seaward.* Atheneum.

Corbett, W. J. 1983. *Song of Pentecost.* *Dutton.

Curry, Jane. 1981. *Wolves of Aam.* *Atheneum.

Dubois, William Penn. 1986. *21 Balloons.* Puffin Books.

Garner, Alan. 1961. *Weirdstone of Brisingamen.* *Walck.

Greaves, Margaret. 1975. *Dagger and the Bird.* Harper.

Hearne, Betsy. 1977. *South Star.* *Atheneum.

Hoban, Russell. 1967. *Mouse and His Child.* Harper.

Jones, Diane. 1981. *Homeward Bounders.* Greenwillow.

Kendall, Carol. 1959. *Gammage Cup.* Harcourt.

L'Engle, Madeline. 1976. *A Wrinkle in Time.* Dell.

Levin, Betty. 1973. *Sword of Culann.* *Macmillan.

Lewis, C. S. 1988. *The Lion, the Witch and the Wardrobe.* *Macmillan.

Lindgren, Astrid. 1983. *Ronia, the Robber's Daughter.* Viking.

Lovett, Margaret. 1967. *Great and Terrible Quest.* Holt.

Martin, Graham. 1981. *Giftwish.* *Houghton Mifflin.

McCaffrey, Anne. 1976. *Dragonsong.* *Atheneum.

McKenzie, Ellen. 1968. *Taash and the Jesters.* *Holt.

McKinley, Robin. 1984. *Hero and the Crown.* Greenwillow.

McNeill, Janet. 1967. *Tom's Tower.* Little.

Nichols, Ruth. 1986. *Walk Out of the World.* Ace.

Norton, Adre. 1965. *Steel Magic.* World.

Service, Pamela. 1975. *Winter of Magic's Return.* *Atheneum.

Snyder, Zilpha Keatley. 1985. *Below the Root.* *Atheneum.

Stearns, Pamela. 1976. *Into the Painted Bear Lair.* Houghton Mifflin.

Steele, Mary. 1969. *Journey Outside.* Viking.

Tannen, Mary. 1982. *Lost Legend of Finn.* *Random.

Tolkein, J. R. R. 1966. *The Hobbitt.* *Houghton Mifflin.

Vande Velde, Vivian. 1985. *Hidden Magic.* Crown.

White, T. H. 1939. *The Sword in the Stone.* Putnam.

Wrede, Patricia. 1993. *Talking to Dragons.* *Harcourt.

Yep, Laurence. 1982. *Dragon of the Lost Sea.* Harper.

Yolen, Jane. 1981. *Acorn Quest.* Crowell.

RESPONSE JOURNALS

Materials

response journals

pencils

Preparation

Make a response journal of ten half sheets of lined paper for each student (see technique 5, Teacher-Made Books, on page 273). If you are unused to response journals be sure to refer to technique 10, Response Journals, on page 281 for an overview of how to ensure the most student involvement.

This activity is designed to stimulate students' thoughtful interaction with the story. It will continue all during the reading of *Abel's Island* and it correlates with lesson 3. On these pages you will find specific activities to do with the response journals after you have read certain story chapters. If other, better questions or activities occur to you, do not hesitate to substitute them for mine. Always be aware, however, of students' need for privacy, of being able to choose whether or not to share life events with you.

Procedure

Step 1: After reading chapter 1, ask students to write about how this book is different from other books they may have read (animal characters), and ask them to list a few other books that they have read in which animals talk and have adventures.

Step 2: After reading chapters 2 and 3, start making a model island using directions in lesson 3. Include a model of the cherry birch tree and the mouse. Emphasize now and throughout these activities that in order to have a fantasy, the author must create the details of a fantasy world, and in order to understand and enjoy the book, the readers must enter into that world and bring it to life. We often imagine these worlds, but with this book we actually will be creating the author's world.

Step 3: After reading chapter 4, do lesson 4.

Step 4: After reading chapter 5, have students write and draw what needs to be added to the island (plants, a stone for Abel to sit on, Amanda's scarf). Then make plans for how to get the items.

Step 5: Have students do the math needed to figure out the actual size of Abel's Island. They will need to measure a real mouse's tail and apply that measurement to Abel's guess of 12,000 tails long and 5,000 tails wide. Measure the size of the boat on your playground. Then ask students to write what they think William Steig had to do before he decided to give those numbers in his book.

Step 6: After reading chapter 6, students write and draw any new elements, such as the log, and the class makes plans to add them to the island.

Optional Step 7: Begin lesson 5, in which students build Abel's city house.

Step 8: After reading chapter 7, you might begin lesson 6. Do not have students write in their response journals.

Step 9: In the middle of chapter 8, just before Abel's letter, ask students to write letters to Amanda as if they were Abel. Remind them to include some directions on how to find him, as well as to express his sentiments and feelings. Then read the rest of the chapter.

Step 10: After reading chapters 9 and 10, have students write and draw what needs to be added (watch, book, clay figures) and make arrangements for doing so. Everyone might work on making one of the small clay elements to add to the island.

Step 11: After reading chapters 11 and 12, ask students to write their thoughts and feelings about Abel's troubles at this point.

Step 12: After reading chapters 13 and 14, have students write about how they feel about being alone and how they deal with loneliness. Some may enjoy being alone; others may not. Discuss their writing as a class.

Step 13: After reading chapter 14, have students figure out how to add a frog, real or imaginary, to the pond. If they choose to add a real frog, they can take turns observing him and writing their observations in their response journals.

Step 14: After reading chapters 15 and 16, have students write their thoughts and feelings about Gower and whether they think he will send help and why.

Step 15: After reading chapter 17, have students draw and add any last elements to the island.

Step 16: After reading chapter 18, have students predict what they think will happen.

Step 17: After reading chapters 19 and 20, ask students to write what they like about the island (and mouse house if you did that, too). Ask them to tell how building their island helped their understanding of the book (metacognition).

Optional Step 18: Ask students to evaluate their response journals according to guidelines in technique 10, Response Journals, on page 281, and then turn them in to you with the evaluation (metacognition).

Multiple Intelligence Connections

FREE READING CHOICES

Materials

books from the literature connections list and any other books that deal with heroic journeys

Preparation

Gather as many books as you can find that are based on the hero's journey pattern (see Literature Connections, page 216, for suggestions).

Procedure

Step 1: Have students read freely in self-directed books for an extended period each day. Also have them report on their reading to the class. See technique 1, Free Reading with Literature Connections, on page 267 for a simple reporting idea.

Step 2: You may want to use the students' individual reading in lesson 9.

Multiple Intelligence Connections

Lesson 3

A REAL ISLAND HOME

This story comes alive for students as they create their own island. There are two ways to do this lesson.

1. One Large Class Island

Materials

everything needed to make a real island in your classroom
 a child's plastic wading pool
 five or six bricks or large rocks
 100 pounds of sand
 five pounds of potting soil
 grass seed
 assorted tree-like plants or sticks

Preparation

Read *Abel's Island* through chapter 3.

Procedure

Step 1: Let students work with you to create the island. Find a place in your room to keep this island. Put the bricks or rocks in the center of the pool and pour the sand in so that the sand on top of the bricks forms the island. Hollow out a part of the island sand for the potting soil. Let it form little hills and valleys. Scatter grass seed on the soil. Slowly add water to the pool, isolating the island, and gently water the grass seeds on the island.

Step 2: As you read each chapter, add story elements to the island as they are described. The birch tree, the hollow log, and later the book and the pocket watch. Students can even add the clay or wood sculptures of Abel's family. (Brown bars of soap can be whittled with a dull knife, or figures can be modeled with clay.)

2. Small Group Islands

Materials

a cardboard base such as the side of a cardboard box or a cardboard pizza round

modeling clay

paper

sticks

branches

assorted art supplies

Preparation

Read *Abel's Island* through chapter 3.

Procedure

Step 1: Divide your class into groups of two to four students. Make each group responsible for creating its own island. Give some suggestions, but let each group use its imagination. Some might use clay only, others cut paper, still others a combination. Students might bring elements from home, such as a crystal mouse or a ceramic frog.

Step 2: After reading the first three chapters, start with students creating just the bare island. As elements are mentioned in the book, the groups can meet and decide how to add these new features to their islands.

Step 3: After the book is finished and the island is completed, ask students to write in the response journals (or on paper, if you are not using response journals) to tell what they like about the island that they created and how building their island helped them understand the book (metacognition).

More Challenge

Step 1: Let students design, create, and try out boats made of natural materials such as the ones Abel made to try to escape.

Step 2: When the frog visits the island, add a real frog instead of a statue for just a day or two. Have students take turns observing and taking notes about the frog's actions. Students could graph how much time it spends sitting, swimming, and doing other activities.

Multiple Intelligence Connections

ABEL'S BOAT

Materials

art paper

pencils

natural elements described in *Abel's Island*

Preparation

Read *Abel's Island* through chapter 4 with you class.

Procedure

Choose one of the following:

Ask students to bring the text to life by drawing a detailed picture of one of the boats that Abel built. You will need to give each student a copy of the description of the boat of his or her choice.

or

Let students design, build, and test boats made from natural elements. They might work in pairs. After testing, have students write paragraphs about their thought processes as they built the boats and their feelings about their results.

Multiple Intelligence Connections

MOUSE HOUSE

Materials

assorted art supplies

several boxes for mouse-house rooms

Preparation

Obtain five or six boxes, wallpaper samples and wrapping paper for walls, carpet samples or construction paper for carpets and tiles. Also gather supplies for making mouse furniture, including toothpicks, bottle-caps, empty matchboxes, empty thread spools, walnut halves, tongue depressors, fabric scraps, and glue. Read at least through chapter 3 of *Abel's Island*.

Procedure

Step 1: Discuss the fact that Abel was a rich mouse and probably lived in an elegant and gracious home. Tell students that while reading this book, they will be invited to find ways to design and make a wonderful mouse house with elegant mouse furniture, so that if Abel ever gets home he will have a lovely home to live in.

Step 2: Suggest that the large boxes could be joined together and modified to make a topless mouse-house for Abelard and Amanda. Work with the class arranging the boxes until the mouse house looks right. Then label each room with what you have decided it should be. Mark where doors and windows should go.

Step 3: Divide the class into five or six groups and give each group one of the boxes to decorate a room in the mouse house. Next, have students cut or draw windows and doors, lay carpet, and paint or paper the walls.

Optional Step 4: Add a math lesson on square footage. Ask each group to submit the measurements and square footage of their walls and floors. Price each carpet or wall covering and have students calculate the cost of their construction.

Step 5: Fasten the rooms together and paint the outside. A removable roof could also be constructed.

Step 6: Bring out a variety of art supplies for the mouse furniture. Challenge students to design the mouse furniture or even mouse transportation. Give students one period to begin work and allow students to continue to work on this project for homework or in their extra time.

Step 7: At the end of the book, when Abel comes home, transfer the toy mouse from the island to the mouse house you have built.

Multiple Intelligence Connections

Lesson 6

CRITICAL ATTRIBUTES OF PLANTS

Materials

pencils

work sheet 9-1, Critical Attributes of Plants

plant name squares found on page 237

Preparation

For each student, duplicate page 237 and cut out the squares along the lines. Read at least through chapter 7 of *Abel's Island*.

Procedure

Step 1: Tell students that they will be trying to guess a rule about the words that you will be showing them. (The first time you play this game, your categories are "edible plants" and "inedible plants.")

Step 2: Prepare a place to show two sets of plant names. This place might be on the floor or pinned to a bulletin board. Make two distinct columns or areas, but do not label them. It will be your students' job to try to figure out what the labels or categories should be.

Step 3: Place one edible plant name in the first column and an inedible plant in the second column. Then show students a third plant name and ask them to predict in which column it will go. (Students can point thumbs or pencils to left or right. Be sure that they all commit at once, on a signal, or they will copy their friends.) After they have voted, place the word in the correct column without a comment.

Step 4: Repeat the procedure with a new plant name. (Refer to the original work sheet 9-1 for the order of presentation.) This time, after students have voted, ask four or five students to explain their theories. Help them clarify with comments such as, "Oh, you have a flowering/nonflowering theory," or "You have a poison/not poison theory." This discussion of student theories is the heart of the lesson. Never indicate whether students have the correct theory; they must prove it for themselves.

Step 5: After this second guess, tell all students that you want them to write their current theories on their papers. Encourage their written responses, as most children hesitate to record a wrong answer. (I circulate and star the papers of students who write a theory until all have done so.) Then tell the class that their theories may be right or wrong, but as soon as each theory is disproved with a new example, each student should cross it out and write a new one.

Step 6: Continue adding plant names, voting, discussing theories, and writing and crossing out hypotheses. There will come a time when most students are fairly certain that their theories are correct. You can invite them to test their hypotheses by asking about a plant name that is not on the list yet. When all are fairly sure, confirm or help refine their theories.

More Challenge

Play this game again another day with a different classification in mind, such as first half or last half of alphabet, two-syllable words or not two-syllable words, plants that provide vegetables or not. Add more plant names from your research in lesson 6. After another session, some students might like to propose a category to try to challenge the class.

Multiple Intelligence Connections

Lesson 7 — EDIBLE PLANT RESEARCH

Materials

encyclopedias

books about edible wild plants

chart paper

drawing paper

pencils

optional: materials to make a large map of the world (or the United States for 5th grade) on a bulletin board

Preparation

Gather books on the topic of edible wild plants that grow in all parts of the world. Read through chapter 7 of *Abel's Island*.

Procedure

Step 1: Discuss how Abel knew what to eat on his island. Tell how this author would need to research to find out which plants are edible before he could put this information in his book. Ask students what might happen if William Steig wrote that a plant was edible when it was actually inedible or poisonous (a reader might eat the plant and get sick).

Step 2: Ask students how they think William Steig could have found out about edible plants. Record the ideas on the board (see example below).

books	experts
encyclopedia	from his childhood

Step 3: Ask students to pretend that they are authors who intend to write a book and decide in which part of the world (or the United States for 5th grade) they want their book to take place. Ask them why location would matter (different plants grow in different geographical areas).

Step 4: Have students work individually, with a partner, or in groups to search through books to find edible plants that grow in their chosen region. Ask students to draw and label the plants with their common names, their scientific names, and descriptions of their tastes if possible.

Optional Step 5: Have some students work on creating a large world or U.S. map on a bulletin board. When other students finish their research and drawing, have them put their plants in the correct region of the map.

Step 6: Have students invent a hero for the book that they are pretending to write. Assuming that their hero is lost in the wilderness, students write a chapter that tells how he or she finds the food the students have researched, prepares it, and eats it. Ask students to describe the touch and taste of the foods.

More Challenge

Since the focus of our unit is on adventures in imaginary worlds, at least some students might prefer to write about a hero in a fantasy setting. If so, ask them to begin by drawing the fantasy plants in the same way that they drew the real ones, including common names, pseudo-scientific names, and descriptions of the taste. Then students can write their segment providing details about the imaginary plants including the tastes and textures for each plant.

Multiple Intelligence Connections

Lesson 8

THE HERO'S JOURNEY

Materials

copies of work sheet 9-2, A Hero's Journey
a transparency or chart of work sheet 9-2

Preparation

Make a copy of work sheet 9-2 for student partners. Also make a transparency from work sheet 9-2 or copy it onto a chart or chalkboard. Finish reading *Abel's Island*.

Procedure

Step 1: Tell students that *Abel's Island* is an example of a certain type of literature known as the hero's journey. In every hero's journey there is a similar pattern of events, and yet every hero learns something a little different from any other.

Step 2: Using a story familiar to most children (for instance, the movie *The Wizard of Oz*), read aloud each item on the work sheet and ask students to help you figure out what part of Dorothy's story matches each basic element (see example on page 227).

Step 3: You can model a second example using an Olympic athlete who wins a gold medal: An ordinary kid from an ordinary town (1) is chosen because she or he has Olympic potential (2). He or she is given a special coach, special practices, special foods (3); faces incredible odds, trials, and contests (4). He or she overcomes all and wins the medal (5) and stands with our flag and the medal that belongs not only to the athlete, but to all of us (6).

Step 4: Give pairs of students a copy of work sheet 9-2 and tell the partners to refer to Abelard's story and complete the work sheet.

Note: Element 3 is not as clear in this story as in many heros' journeys. Students might decide on the birch tree and the hollow log as special friends, or on Abelard's remembered botany book, or even on his great determination and quick wits. Also, element 6 is not clearly stated at the end, but throughout the book we see Abel's transformation from a rich city mouse to one who enjoys living by his wits and eating wild plants.

Step 5: When work sheets are finished, discuss students' answers. Then give partners some time to add to or revise their opinions; have both sign the paper and hand it in.

Multiple Intelligence Connections

Example Worksheet 9-2
A Hero's Journey

1. A hero who represents ordinary people is selected.

   Dorothy is just like all of us who are bored at home and want to go "over the rainbow."

2. The hero passes through a magic doorway (via an unusual event) into a different world.

   A tornado picks up Dorothy's house and deposits it in Oz.

3. The hero is given special friends or magic powers to help him or her win the prize.

   The Tin Woodsman, the Cowardly Lion, and the Scarecrow join Dorothy, and the magic slippers protect her.

4. The hero struggles against terrible obstacles, a struggle that seems hopeless at times.

   Dorothy fights talking trees, poppies that put her to sleep, and the Wicked Witch of the West. Even the Great and Powerful Wizard of Oz lets her down.

5. The hero finally wins.

   Dorothy melts the witch, clicks her heels together, and goes home.

6. The hero is transformed and tells others what he or she has learned.

   Dorothy says, "There's no place like home, there's no place like home."

Lesson 9

MORE HEROES' JOURNEYS

Materials

an assortment of books from the literature connections list

copies of work sheet 9-2, A Hero's Journey

pencils

Preparation

Do lesson 8. Finish reading *Abel's Island*. Have each student read one of the books from the literature connections list. Students can be reading the books on their own time while you are reading *Abel's Island* to the whole class. After the books have been read and the class has finished lesson 8, ask all students to fill out a copy of work sheet 9-2 using their books they read on their own. The work sheet helps students understand the pattern behind this genre of literature.

Procedure

After the assignment is completed, have students give oral reports about their books, telling only about elements 1 through 4 and leaving their classmates in suspense about the endings. (This change stimulates interest and sells the books to the class.)

More Challenge

As students finish reading their independent selections, invite them to prepare a book presentation or book report. See technique 12, Thoughtful Book Reports, on page 284 for creative book report ideas.

Multiple Intelligence Connections

COMPARE WITH BEAUTY AND THE BEAST

Materials

copies of work sheet 9-3, Venn Diagram, for students

a videotape of Walt Disney's *Beauty and the Beast* or a copy of any version of that story

an overhead transparency or a chart made from work sheet 9-2, A Hero's Journey

Preparation

Read all of *Abel's Island* and view or read a version of *Beauty and the Beast*. Make an overhead transparency or chart from work sheet 9-2 and one of work sheet 9-3. Also duplicate work sheet 9-3 for each student.

Procedure

Step 1: To stimulate students' thinking, ask them to help you fill in work sheet 9-2 based on *Beauty and the Beast*.

Step 2: Give students copies of work sheet 9-3 and tell them to label one circle "Beauty" and the other circle "Abel." Ask students to write about the characters' circumstances and their actions.

Step 3: Students might work with partners to help each other complete the task of comparing the two stories. Tell students that you do not want them to put each little event that happened in the stories, but that you want them to compare similar story events (see example on page 230).

Step 4: After students have worked on their individual Venn diagrams for a while, ask them to tell you their ideas so that you can make a large chart of everyone's ideas. Do not record every insignificant detail, such as boy or girl, island or castle, but write in the main story elements.

Step 5: Ask students to turn their papers over and explain to you why they think that there were so many similarities in these two stories. We hope they will see how these two stories are from the same literary genre and so have at least six elements in common. Beaut's sixth element is learning that outward appearance is not as important as true character.

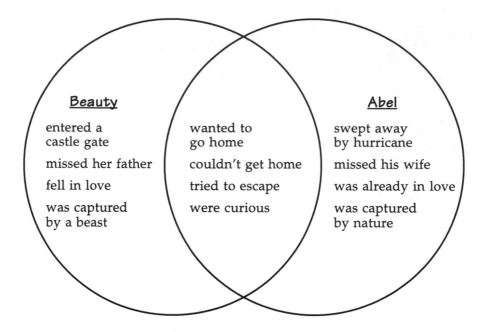

Beauty		Abel
entered a castle gate	wanted to go home	swept away by hurricane
missed her father	couldn't get home	missed his wife
fell in love	tried to escape	was already in love
was captured by a beast	were curious	was captured by nature

Multiple Intelligence Connections

Lesson 11

WRITING YOUR OWN HERO'S JOURNEY

Materials

overhead transparency or chart of work sheet 9-2, A Hero's Journey

writing and drawing paper

pencils

other materials for illustrating

Preparation

Finish reading *Abel's Island* and do lesson 8.

Procedure

Step 1: Give students six pages of paper for taking notes of their story ideas. Tell the class that they will each be writing a hero's journey of their own.

Step 2: Using your transparency or chart as a model, students write one of the six elements of a hero's journey at the top of each page.

Step 3: Ask students to close their eyes and imagine what kind of hero they would like to write about. If they enjoyed Abel or the heros from their own books, they could write another adventure for that character. Or they could imagine a time traveler, a future space traveler, or another special character.

Step 4: Ask the students to continue imagining until they can think of an event that would hurl their hero into another world. The event could be natural, such as a tornado, a hurricane, an earthquake; or a fantasy such as a midnight visit from an elf or a glimpse of a unicorn or a leprechaun.

Step 5: Give students time to think and decide and then change their minds about these two elements. Then students should record their decisions on the first two sheets of paper.

Step 6: Take the class through the rest of this process, always giving them time to close their eyes and imagine what might happen to their hero in terms of each of the story elements. After each period of thinking and imagining, students write their ideas in rough form on each of the seven sheets. Encourage students to help others think of creative options, but let each author make the final decisions.

Step 7: After all six sheets are finished, students use these notes to write their stories. Extend this activity as far as you wish, depending on the quality of the stories and the enthusiasm of your students. You might include peer editing, revision, and a final published book with illustrations. You might have students visit another class and read their stories to younger students.

Step 8: When the stories are completed, ask students to write paragraphs that tell you what they like about their story and what helped them to do such a good job (metacognition).

Suggestions for Simplifying

Have students for whom this lesson might be too difficult take the story of Abel and rewrite it themselves, as if Abel were telling his story to Amanda. Or they can imagine that Abel runs into trouble again and has a second adventure, perhaps by accidentally boarding a train, an automobile, or a rocket ship.

More Challenge

Do lesson 12.

Multiple Intelligence Connections

Lesson 12

PERSONIFICATION

Materials

copies of the text of *Abel's Island*

Preparation

With your class, read *Abel's Island*.

Procedure

Step 1: Show students several examples of personification, such as "the wind screamed" or "the tree shook its branches."

Step 2: Challenge pairs of students to look through the text of *Abel's Island* to find more examples of personification. Have them draw one or two of their favorites.

Optional Step 3: Ask students to add several examples of personification to their own rough drafts of their heroes' journeys from lesson 11.

Multiple Intelligence Connections

HEROIC MUSIC

Materials

songs and orchestral music based on heroism

Preparation

Gather ballads and other music based on heroes, such as "John Henry," "Guantanamera," or "Underground Railway."

Procedure

Introduce and teach students the songs (see technique 3, Music Connections, for suggestions). With orchestral selections that are based on heroic actions, such as *The William Tell Overture,* tell students the story and let them listen to the music while creating mental images of the action. After listening, students can discuss some of their images, then express them in an art medium such as drawing, painting, sculpture, or dance.

More Challenge

Students write a new heroic song, perhaps about Abelard or Amanda. They may use the tune of one of the songs you introduced in this lesson.

Unit 9

MATERIALS

Work Sheet 9-1

Critical Attributes of Plants

The plants in the left-hand column are edible; those in the right-hand column are not edible. All are listed in the approximate order I recommend you present them; it is an order that will encourage students to make guesses that may be incorrect so that they have the opportunity to form and test several hypotheses. When presenting the plant names to your class, vary the order of edible and inedible plants; otherwise, students will form their guesses merely on which column is due next. For instance, present one edible, two inedible, two edible, one inedible, and so on.

EDIBLE	NOT EDIBLE
rose petals	crabgrass
Joshua tree buds	milkweed
lettuce leaves	poison oak
watercress leaves	oleander
fern tips	foxglove
yucca flowers	ivy
California bay leaves	azaleas
carrots	holly
apples	hemlock
wild onions	hydrangea
tomatoes	tomato leaves
acorns	daffodil bulbs
choke cherries	hyacinth
wild grapes	poison ivy

Work Sheet 9-2

A Hero's Journey

1. A hero who represents ordinary people is selected.

_____

_____

_____

_____

2. The hero passes through a magic doorway (via an unusual event) into a different world.

_____

_____

_____

_____

3. The hero is given special friends or magic powers to help him or her win the prize.

_____

_____

_____

_____

4. The hero struggles against terrible obstacles, a struggle that seems hopeless at times.

_____

_____

_____

_____

5. The hero finally wins.

_____

_____

_____

_____

6. The hero is transformed and tells others what he or she has learned.

_____

_____

_____

_____

Work Sheet 9-3

Venn Diagram

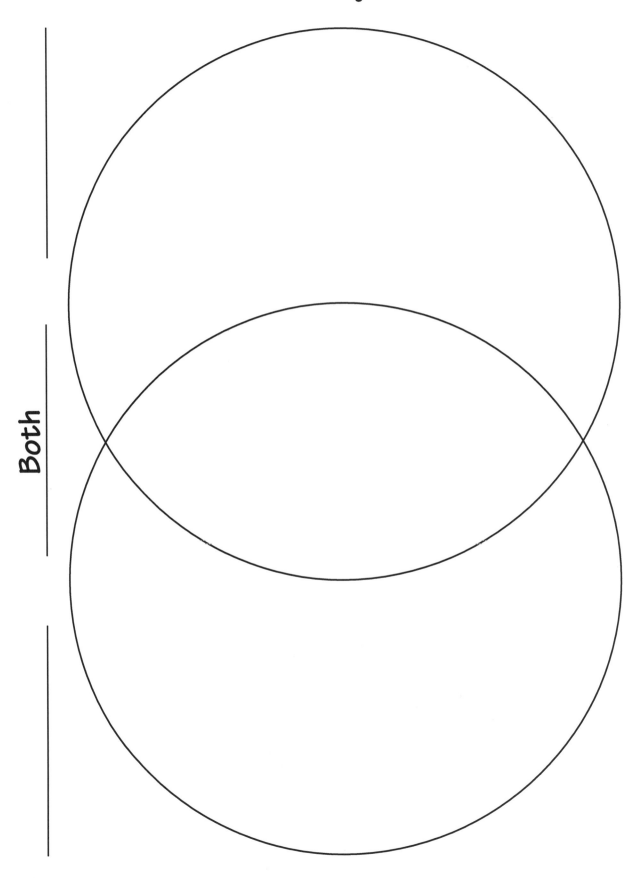

Both

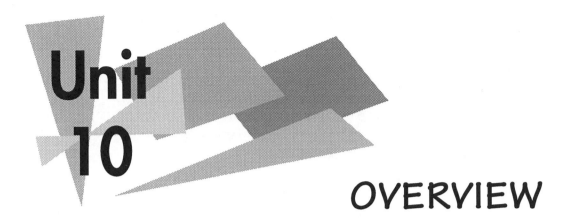

Unit 10

OVERVIEW

Central Literature Selection:
Where the Red Fern Grows
by Wilson Rawls

Unit Focus:
Pet Ownership
Grades: 5–6

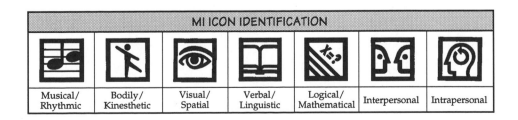

THINKING SKILLS SYMBOLS IDENTIFICATION				
Personal Connection	Creation	Mastery	Reasoning	Metacognition

MI ICON IDENTIFICATION						
Musical/ Rhythmic	Bodily/ Kinesthetic	Visual/ Spatial	Verbal/ Linguistic	Logical/ Mathematical	Interpersonal	Intrapersonal

Lesson 1: **Response Journals** (Grades 5–6; five minutes or more each day)

As the chapters are read, students make thoughtful responses in a teacher-made book.

Lesson 2: **Free Reading with Literature Connections** (Grades 5–6; twenty to thirty minutes each day)

Students select a book from the literature connections list or any other book about pet ownership to read independently, make brief oral reports to the class, and write an optional book report.

Lesson 3: **Saving Money** (Grades 5–6; one class period)

This is both a math activity and an exercise in appreciation of commitment as students problem solve to discover how much work they would have to do to buy Billy's coon hounds with today's dollar.

Lesson 4: **Pet Bulletin Board and Scrapbooks** (Grades 5–6; homework and one or more class periods)

Students bring pictures and write detailed descriptions of their own past, present, and possibly future pets.

Lesson 5: **Pet Research** (Grades 5–6; several class periods)

This lesson is designed to teach students how to do research. After the teacher models one entire research project, students pick a pet to research on their own.

Lesson 6: **Guesses and Facts Double Entry** (Grades 5–6; one class period)

This highly motivational technique helps students develop an interest in learning new facts and information.

Lesson 7: **Appalachian Music** (Grades 5–6; three to five class periods)

Students enjoy and participate in bluegrass music. They make and play some simple instruments.

Lesson 8: **Veterinary Visit** (Grades 5–6; two class periods)

Students prepare questions to ask a veterinarian, either in a classroom visit or on a field trip.

Lesson 9: **Comparing the Book and a Movie** (Grades 5–6; three or more class periods)

Use Venn diagrams to compare the book with the film version.

Lesson 10: **Joys and Burdens** (Grades 5–6; one or two class periods)

After reading reports on pet care, students list joys and burdens of pet ownership and write an opinion paper about whether pet ownership is worthwhile.

Synopsis of *Where the Red Fern Grows*

This is a thrilling story about a poor mountain boy who saves his money to buy his heart's desire: two expensive coon hounds. Together they roam the hills of Cherokee County, meeting adventure and trouble. The book depicts transcendent love of a boy and his dogs. True-to-life details of coon hunting and even the accidental death of a neighborhood bully are included. The story ends with the gory death of the two beloved and faithful dogs, but after his tears Billy is touched with a miracle of love and faith as the dogs' graves are blessed with the sacred red fern that legend tells him can be planted only by angels.

Explanation of Unit Focus: Pet Ownership

This unit asks students to think about the pleasures and responsibilities of pet ownership. As they read other books about children and their pets, students will learn about the variety of pets and the responsibility that goes with pet ownership. They will reflect on their own adventures with pets and see the world through their animals' eyes.

Cross-Curricular Connections

This unit might correlate with the study of animal behavior and even some learning about how to train animals with positive reinforcement. Another science match would be with any study of the needs of animals, the different classes of animals, and how herbivores, carnivores, and omnivores fit into the food chain. It will also fit in with a study of the history of the United States, and Billy's mountains can be located on a map.

Response Journals

The response journal is a project that spans the reading of the book and serves to organize your unit. If you do not choose to do the journals, you can still do any of the other lessons and select a few of the suggested response journal activities without doing the whole project.

To Start the Unit

Look at the suggested lessons and select those that are appropriate for your class. If you decide to use response journals, distribute the teacher-made journals and then read the first two chapters of *Where the Red Fern Grows* aloud to your class. If you have a class set of *Where the Red Fern Grows*, assign the first two chapters, being sure that students who cannot read it on their own are helped in some way to keep up with the rest of the class. If you do not wish to do response journals, read *Where the Red Fern Grows* aloud to your students, stopping after each appropriate chapter to engage in the lessons you select.

Literature Connections

Following is a list of books on the unit's focus for your students to read independently during the unit and even after you have finished the unit. If each student is reading a different book, discussions and activities regarding the unit's focus will be far richer than if everyone reads the same selection. See technique 1, Free Reading with Literature Connections, for suggestions.

Books

Alexander, Lloyd. 1963. *Time Cat.* Holt, Rinehart, and Winston.

Angell, Judie. 1984. *A Home Is to Share and Share and Share.* Bradbury.

Armstrong, William, H. 1969. *Sounder.* Harper.

Butterworth, Oliver. 1956. *The Enormous Egg.* Little.

Callen, Larry. 1976. *Pinch.* Little.

Cleary, Bruce. 1991. *Jeremy Thatcher, Dragon Hatcher.* Harcourt.

Dana, Barbara. 1982. *Zucchini.* Harper.

Farley, Walter. 1946. *The Black Stallion.* Random.

Fleischman, Sid. 1992. *Jim Ugly.* Greenwillow.

Gardiner, John. 1983. *Stone Fox.* Harper.

Gipson, Fred. 1956. *Old Yeller.* Harper.

Graeber, Charlotte. 1988. *Mustard.* Bantam.

Johnston, Johanna. 1989. *Great Gravity the Cat.* Shoe String.

King-Smith, Dick. 1993. *The Cuckoo Child.* Hyperion.

Knight, Eric. 1992. *Lassie, Come Home.* Dell.

Morey, Walt. 1965. *Gentle Ben.* Dutton.

Naylor, Phyllis. 1991. *Shiloh.* Atheneum.

North, Sterling. 1963. *Rascal: A Memoir of a Better Era.* Dutton.

O'Hara, Mary. 1941. *My Friend Flicka.* Lippincott.

Pearce, Philippa. 1979. *Battle of Bubble and Squeak.* Deutsche.

Peck, Robert Newton. 1972. *A Day No Pigs Would Die.* Knopf.

Rawlings, Marjorie Kinnan. 1939. *The Yearling.* Scribner.

Sargent, Sara. 1981. *Weird Henry Berg.* Dell.

Selden, George. 1993. *Cricket in Times Square.* Dell.

Sherlock, Patti. 1992. *Some Fine Dog.* Holiday.

Springer, Nancy. 1989. *They're All Named Wildfire.* Macmillan.

Taylor, Theodore. 1989. *The Trouble with Tuck.* Doubleday.

Van Steenwyk, Elizabeth. 1987. *Three Dog Winter.* Walker.

Wagner, Jane. 1972. *J. T.* Dell.

Wallace, E. B. 1988. *Beauty.* Holiday.

White, E. B. 1952. *Charlotte's Web.* Harper.

RESPONSE JOURNALS

Materials

teacher-made books

pencils

Preparation

Make books for each student with about 10 lined pages (see technique 5, Teacher-Made Books, on page 273). If you are unfamiliar with using response journals, read technique 10, Response Journals, on page 280 for an overview of how to ensure the most student involvement.

This activity is designed to stimulate students' thoughtful interaction with the story and will continue all during the reading of *Where the Red Fern Grows*. On these pages you will find specific activities to do with the response journals after certain story chapters. If other, better questions or activities occur to you, do not hesitate to substitute them for mine. Always be aware, however, of students' need for privacy, of being able to choose whether or not to share life events with you.

Procedure

Step 1: After reading chapters 1 and 2, have students write their thoughts and feelings about Billy's wanting some coon dogs so badly that he cannot sleep. Or have students recall a time when they wanted something that much, or have them talk about their reactions to Billy's longing.

Step 2: After reading chapter 3, have students write their thoughts and feelings about Billy's saving for two years to buy those dogs. They might also tell of a time that they saved money for something very important to them. You could follow with lesson 3.

Step 3: After reading chapter 4, ask students to close their eyes and remember a time when they just couldn't wait for something to come, such as a package in the mail, a visit from a friend or relative, or just a special day. Give them a minute to remember how they felt and then write about it.

Step 4: After reading chapter 5, have students record any thoughts or feelings about what happens to Billy in this chapter.

Step 5: Before reading chapter 6, have the class open their response journals. While you are reading have them listen for something that reminds them of an event or a moment in their own lives. As soon as they hear it, students should record their memories. At the end of the chapter, ask volunteer students to tell about the event in their lives that is like a part of Billy's story.

Step 6: After reading chapter 7, do lesson 7.

Step 7: After reading chapter 8, have students predict whether or not Billy will cut this tree down all by himself and give their reasons for their predictions. Have partners share their predictions with each other, then with the whole class. You might make a graph of the different predictions.

Step 8: After reading chapter 9, have students write their own thoughts and feelings about Billy's success in toppling the tree. Are they glad or not? Why do they think the wind touched only that tree?

Step 9: After reading chapter 10, discuss the differences in personality between the two dogs Little Ann and Old Dan, and ask students to share personalities of pets that they have known. List some characteristics of their pets on a chart or bulletin board. Then have students write about the personality of an animal that they have known. If they have not known one personally, let them write about a television animal.

Step 10: After reading chapter 11, do lesson 5.

Step 11: After reading chapter 12, have students start lesson 6. Do not have them write in their response journals.

Step 12: After reading chapter 13, hold a class discussion on why students think the author had Rubin fall on the ax and die. What did that event add to the story? Then have students write about their thoughts and feelings about this story element. Do they agree that it was an important part of the story? Why do they think Rawls included it?

Step 13: After reading chapter 14, have students tell their thoughts and feelings about the bet and Rubin's death.

Step 14: After reading chapter 15, have students write about things that they have heard that cause bad luck and then talk to partners about their lists. Then the class discusses what they think about the idea of bad luck.

Step 15: After reading chapters 16, 17, and 18, have students write about their reactions to the contest. If they have ever been in a contest or won one, they might tell about their own experiences.

Step 16: After reading chapters 19 and 20, ask students to write why they think Rawls called the whole book *Where the Red Fern Grows* when the book has only a tiny little bit about a red fern. Then have them discuss their responses with partners and with the whole class. Do lesson 9.

Multiple Intelligence Connections

Lesson 2
FREE READING WITH LITERATURE CONNECTIONS

Materials

books from the literature connections list and any other books you can gather that deal with pet ownership or pet adventures

Preparation

Gather as many books on this subject as you can find (see Literature Connections, page 244, for suggestions).

Procedure

Have students read freely in self-selected books for an extended period each day. Also have them report to the class in some way. See technique 1, Free Reading with Literature Connections, on page 267 for details. See technique 12 for additional ideas.

Multiple Intelligence Connections

Lesson 3

SAVING MONEY

Materials

paper
pencils
fact sheet 10-1, Money Table

Preparation

Read the first few chapters of *Where the Red Fern Grows*.

Procedure

Step 1: Ask students how much money Billy had to earn and save in order to buy the coon hounds ($50.00).

Step 2: Ask students to help figure out approximately when Billy bought his hounds. (In the book, published in 1961, Rawls was writing about his own childhood. Ask students to watch for other clues about the year as you read through the book together.)

Step 3: Consult the money table on page 259 for the year that you decide on to find out what $1.00 in that year would be worth today. Have students figure out how to find out what those hounds would cost today.

Step 4: Now ask students to imagine an allowance of $5.00 a week for doing chores, and yearly birthday and holiday gifts of $100.00. Have them figure out how long it would take to save enough money to buy the hounds.

More Challenge

Ask students to find out how much a paper route pays, how much mowing lawns pays, and how much baby-sitting pays, and determine how many hours they would have to work to buy the hounds with today's money. Or have them figure out the cost of keeping their own pet(s). They will need to find the price of pet food, measure out bowlfuls to see how many individual meals are in the package, and then figure the cost per day, per week, per month, per year. They could add in costs of shots, license, collars, leashes, and other incidentals. They might call the local animal shelter to find out the shelter's estimate of the cost of keeping different pets.

Multiple Intelligence Connections

Lesson 4

PET BULLETIN BOARD AND SCRAPBOOKS

Note: Students who have never had a pet can use a friend's pet, a classroom pet, or the pet that they are reading about. Students without pictures can draw them or cut pictures of similar animals out of magazines.

Materials

paper

pencils

a blank bulletin board

Preparation

Have students read at least a few chapters of their pet adventure books.

Procedure

Step 1: Ask students to make lists of all of the pets they have ever owned. You may choose to use these lists to make a class graph.

Step 2: Set aside a bulletin board where students can post pictures of their pets, past and present, along with descriptions. Have your class decide what should be in the descriptions (see example on page 248).

Step 3: Invite students to bring to school pictures of any pets that they have owned. Have them copy the categories in the descriptor so that they can fill it out for homework. They may need to ask parents some of the details.

Step 4: Help students figure out how to figure out the pet's weight and height. Discuss this problem with the class. For instance, how would you get a fish's weight? Let the class help you find solutions, emphasizing kind treatment of animals.

Step 5: Let students post their pets' pictures on the bulletin board.

MY FAVORITE PET

NAME: _____

BORN: _____

BREED: _____

COLORS: _____

WEIGHT: _____

HEIGHT: _____

LENGTH: _____

PARENTS: _____

HOW I GOT THIS PET: _____

_____

FAVORITE FOOD: _____

FAVORITE TOY: _____

FAVORITE ACTIVITY: _____

MOST LIKABLE TRAIT: _____

More Challenge

Students make individual scrapbooks with a page for every pet that they have ever owned, and perhaps a few pages for pets they would like to own some day. The class can decide what should be on each page, perhaps the descriptor and picture from the bulletin board and an anecdote about the pet.

Multiple Intelligence Connections

Lesson 5

PET RESEARCH

Materials

an overhead transparency of work sheet 10-1, Webbing

copies of work sheet 10-1

books with information about the lives and care of various pets

books with information about various kinds of pets

Preparation

Make an overhead transparency of work sheet 10-1 or draw a large version of the work sheet on a chart or chalkboard. Gather factual books that will give students information about the lives and the care of various pets.

Procedure

Step 1: Do one research project together so that students all understand the steps necessary. Choose a pet that no one in your classroom happens to own.

Step 2: Use technique 13, Webbing for Research Reports, to get all of the questions that you might wish to answer. Include questions about how to feed and care for the pet, what environment it needs for good health, as well as questions about the length of its life and reproduction cycle. If you have too many important questions to fit on the work sheet, give everyone a second copy and put the rest of the questions there.

Step 3: Once you record the questions, give students the books about pets and ask them to read until someone finds the answer to one of the questions. As soon as someone does, ask him or her to read the information to the class.

Step 4: Using an overhead or a large reproduction of work sheet 10-1, show students how to record their facts on the arms that radiate from the question bubbles. Continue this way until all questions are answered (this step may take more than one class period).

Step 5: After all of the questions are answered and recorded on your model and on the students' work sheets, show students how to expand work sheet 10-1 into a research paper.

Steps to Writing a Research Paper from a Web

1. Decide on the order of the questions and number each bubble accordingly.
2. Write an introductory paragraph that tells what the whole paper will be about.
3. Write one paragraph for each of the question bubbles.
4. Write a closing paragraph that summarizes the paper.

Step 6: Model the beginning paragraph and the first paragraph of the body of the paper, and let the students take over from there with each writing his or her own version of the research paper.

Optional Step 7: Show students how to prepare a bibliography and have them do one for this paper.

More Challenge

Step 1: Now that students know how to write a research paper about pets, have each student choose a pet to research, either one that they own or one that they would someday like to own. Have them follow the same framework, starting with some of the questions that were asked and answered on the model, but adding some of their own special interests. Illustrations and a title page might also be added.

Step 2: While students are working on this individual research project, have them set daily goals using work sheet 10-2, Intentions and Reflections (metacognition). This simple step helps students stay on task on a long project.

Multiple Intelligence Connections

Lesson 6

GUESSES AND FACTS DOUBLE ENTRY

Materials

lined paper

fact sheet 10-2, Raccoons

pencils

Preparation

Read through chapter 7 of *Where the Red Fern Grows*.

Procedure

Step 1: Have students fold their papers in half lengthwise, open the sheet, and trace a line down the center fold. On every other line down the left-hand edge, they will write the numbers from 1 to 10.

Step 2: Label the left column "guesses" and the right column "facts."

Step 3: Ask students to answer the questions on fact sheet 10-2 with their best guesses and write that answer in the "guesses" column. Reassure students that you do not expect them to know all of the correct answers at this point, but that they must make some responses. Encourage and reward their guesses in this step of the lesson, because your best students often have the most trouble recording an answer of which they are not sure.

Step 4: Now read fact sheet 10-2, Raccoons; tell students to raise their hands whenever they hear an answer to one of the questions. Students should either mark their guesses correct or draw lines through the incorrect guesses and write the correct answers directly across on their papers (see example below).

Guesses	Facts
1. Yes C	
2. ~~30 years~~	14 years
3. ~~Yes~~	No

Step 5: As you read the fact sheet and stop to let students write the answers, discuss the information and accept all correct answers in the guess column whether or not they are stated in the fact sheet. Because students have committed themselves to guesses, they are far more interested in learning the correct information than they might be if they just read it without this technique.

Step 6: After all of the questions have been discussed and corrected, students turn their papers in for an *A* if all of the answers were either initially correct or crossed out and corrected.

Optional Step 7: Have students turn their papers over and tell you what they see as the benefits of this kind of lesson (metacognition).

More Challenge

Repeat this technique with short information articles on any topic in which students have some background.

Multiple Intelligence Connections

Lesson 7

APPALACHIAN MUSIC

Materials

recordings of bluegrass music or live bluegrass musicians and dancers, especially songs about dogs

a book on how to make and play simple bluegrass instruments

materials for making the instruments

optional: 1 copy of work sheet 10-2, Intentions and Reflections, page 261, for each student

Preparation

Read at least half of *Where the Red Fern Grows*. Gather recordings or arrange for bluegrass musicians to visit your classroom. Look for contra dancers or other line dancers in your area. Find a book that tells how to make simple instruments and gather the appropriate materials.

Procedure

Step 1: If you recruit live musicians, let them play and let students ask them questions about their music. Perhaps they will teach the students some dances. Or play some recordings for your class.

Step 2: Show students how to make the instruments. Students might work in cooperative groups to make various instruments. If this process will take more than one class period, students can use work sheet 10-2 to help them stay on task.

Step 3: Students play their instruments along with recordings and create their own music.

Multiple Intelligence Connections

VETERINARY VISIT

Materials for Students

paper

pencil

Material for the Teacher

chart paper

Preparation

Read at least some of *Where the Red Fern Grows*. Arrange either for a field trip to a veterinary hospital or for a veterinarian to visit your classroom. Ask the veterinarian to prepare to talk about the variety of pets, the responsibility of pet ownership, and the science and math training required to be a veterinarian.

Procedure

Step 1: Before the field trip or veterinarian visit, prepare your class:

Ask students to write in response journals or on sheets of paper any questions they might ask the veterinarian.

Have pairs of students share their questions with each other and write down any others that they think of.

From these lists, create a whole class list and record it on a large chart.

As a class, decide which questions will be asked. Give the task of asking the questions to the individuals who thought of them on the original lists.

Step 2: After the veterinarian presents her or his information, let students ask the prepared questions.

Step 3: When the interchange is over, ask students to write five bits of information that they learned from this visit (metacognition). Then ask students to share aloud some of these insights.

Multiple Intelligence Connections

COMPARING THE BOOK AND A MOVIE

Materials

a movie version of *Where the Red Fern Grows*

an overhead transparency of work sheet 10-3, Venn Diagram

one copy of work sheet 10-3 for every student

Preparation

Finish reading *Where the Red Fern Grows*. Obtain a movie version of *Where the Red Fern Grows*. Make an overhead transparency or a similar chart from work sheet 10-3 and duplicate the work sheet for every student.

Procedure

Step 1: Before viewing the movie, remind your students that a movie does not have room for every part of the book it portrays. Ask students to write which parts they think will be left out of *Where the Red Fern Grows*. Also ask them to tell which part they would have left out if they were creating a film version.

Step 2: Show the film.

Step 3: Ask students to add to their previous comments to tell their thoughts and feelings about what was left out or changed.

Step 4: Label your copy of work sheet 10-3 with "movie version" on one circle and "book version" on the other.

Step 5: Let students work on their own copies for ten minutes or so and then ask them to help you fill in yours with their ideas. Give students a chance to process their ideas before writing.

Step 6: Ask students to write approximately one page expressing their thoughts and feelings about the differences and similarities between the book and the movie. Remind your students to refer to the class's Venn diagram for further ideas and to be sure to give reasons and explanations for their opinions.

Multiple Intelligence Connections

Lesson 10

JOYS AND BURDENS

Materials

paper or response journals

pencils

Preparation

Do this lesson last, after you have finished reading *Where the Red Fern Grows* and any other lessons you have chosen.

Procedure

Step 1: Ask students to draw a line down the centers of their papers or turn to two facing blank pages in the response journals. They will label one page of the journal "joys" and the other page "burdens."

Step 2: Tell students to make their own lists for a few minutes and then share with partners and add to their lists.

Step 3: From the students' responses, create a master list on a chart or chalkboard.

Step 4: Using technique 11, Writing Opinion Papers (found on page 282), ask students to write an opinion paper taking one of the following stances:

Even though there are burdens in owning a pet, I think it is worth those burdens.

Even though there are benefits in owning a pet, I don't think it is worth the burdens.

I think that only people who are willing to do all the work to keep their pets healthy and happy should have pets.

Multiple Intelligence Connections

Unit
10

MATERIALS

Fact Sheet 10-1
Money Table

Most things that cost $1.00 in 1985 ....would have cost about $1.25 in 1990.

Most things that cost $1.00 in 1980 ....would have cost about $1.75 in 1990.

Most things that cost $1.00 in 1975 ....would have cost about $3.50 in 1990.

Most things that cost $1.00 in 1970 ....would have cost about $6.40 in 1990.

Most things that cost $1.00 in 1965 ....would have cost about $8.00 in 1990.

Most things that cost $1.00 in 1960 ....would have cost about $9.40 in 1990.

Most things that cost $1.00 in 1955 ....would have cost about $10.50 in 1990.

Most things that cost $1.00 in 1950 ....would have cost about $13.25 in 1990.

Most things that cost $1.00 in 1945 ....would have cost about $18.25 in 1990.

Most things that cost $1.00 in 1940 ....would have cost about $26.50 in 1990.

Most things that cost $1.00 in 1935 ....would have cost about $36.32 in 1990.

Most things that cost $1.00 in 1930 ....would have cost about $32.75 in 1990.

Most things that cost $1.00 in 1925 ....would have cost about $24.40 in 1990.

Most things that cost $1.00 in 1920 ....would have cost about $16.10 in 1990.

Most things that cost $1.00 in 1915 ....would have cost about $31.70 in 1990.

Most things that cost $1.00 from 1885–1910 would have cost about $42.00 in 1990.

Most things that cost $1.00 from 1860–1884 would have cost about $31.00 in 1990.

Note: These figures are loosely based on the U.S. Government's Composite Commodity Price Index. They do not take into account the increase in average wages over the years in question but are merely based on the actual price of goods sold.

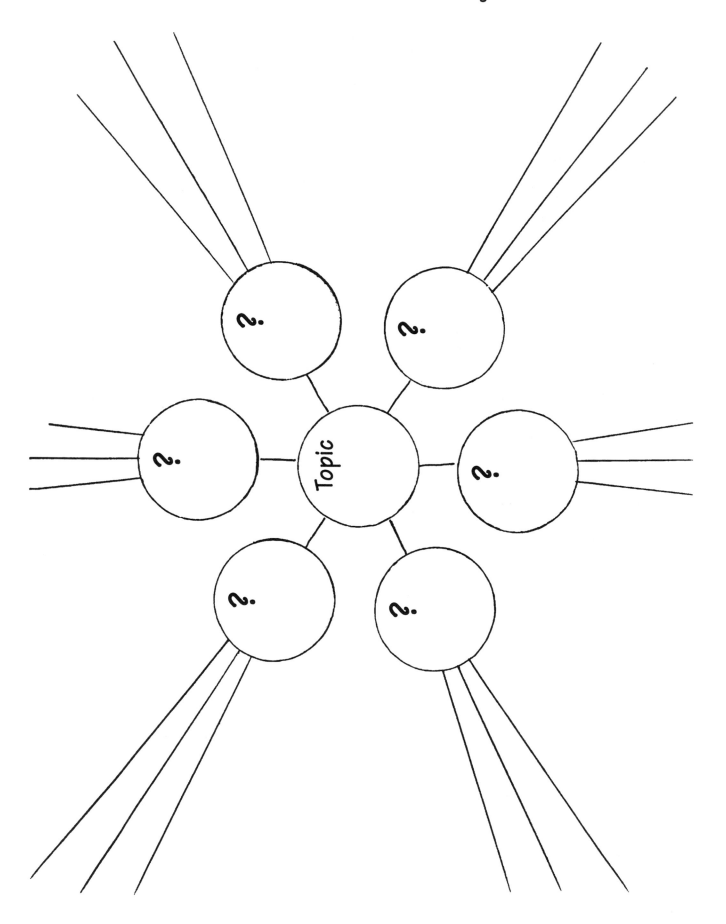

Work Sheet 10-2
Intentions and Reflections
Adding Metacognition to Projects

Date:_____ Today I intend to _____

_____

_____

_____

_____

During this work period, I was able to _____

_____

_____

Tomorrow I hope to

_____

_____

- -

Date:_____ Today I intend to _____

_____

_____

_____

_____

During this work period, I was able to _____

_____

_____

Tomorrow I hope to

_____

_____

- -

Note: For longer projects use additional sheets or have students use a teacher-made journal to make similar daily entries.

Developing Intelligences through Literature © 1996 Zephyr Press, Tucson, AZ

Fact Sheet 10-2

Questions to Ask Before Reading Fact Sheet 10-2

Pause after each question to allow students time to jot down their answers.

1. Do raccoons like to eat the same kind of food as humans?
2. How old can a raccoon live to be in captivity?
3. Do raccoons always wash their food if they can?
4. When a raccoon goes fishing, what does it use for bait?
5. Why was a raccoon arrested in Greely, Colorado?
6. How many babies does a mother raccoon have?
7. Is a raccoon more closely related to a bear, a panda, or a weasel?
8. Are raccoons gentle or fierce?
9. Do raccoons like to play?
10. In a fight with a dog its size, which would be more likely to win?

Fact Sheet 10-2

Raccoons

The raccoon is a sturdy little survivor who is found in every state but Hawaii and can adapt to almost any situation. He prefers to live in wooded areas, but because he is an omnivore, he can adapt to life even in the middle of a city, eating out of humans' garbage cans and raiding their pets' food dishes. Many a dog has had a rude surprise to find his dinner stolen by a fierce little bandit. In a fight, a raccoon can usually beat a dog twice its size.

Even though raccoons can be very fierce when cornered, they also have a gentle side. Many people have made pets of them, although they tend to be tricky to handle in a house.

The raccoon is easily recognized by his mask and bushy tail. Once, in Greely, Colorado, one was mistaken for a burglar peering into a woman's bedroom window. The police were called, and the raccoon was arrested and taken to the nearest humane shelter.

A raccoon's fingers, long and delicate with claws on the ends, have earned him his American Indian–given name of "he who scratches with his hands." He is even able to fish with his long fingers, dabbling one into a stream until a crayfish bites it. As soon as the crayfish takes hold, the raccoon quickly grabs it and eats it.

Raccoons are good climbers and prefer to build their homes in hollow branches high in trees. There they raise their babies; each mother raccoon bears from three to six every year. The babies are born with masks and fur, but they are unable to open their eyes until eighteen days after their birth. Within five or six weeks they are off hunting with their parents, scrambling up and down their home trees with the grace of squirrels.

Raccoons have often been hunted because of their beautiful and durable fur coats. The pioneers made raccoon hats with the tails hanging down. Raccoon skins were even traded for money in early pioneer days. People sometimes earned their living in raccoon hides. Many pioneers ate raccoons, which taste something like the dark meat of a chicken.

There are over thirty varieties of raccoon, and they are related in the Americas to ringtails, coati mundis, and kinkajous. The panda in far-off China is also a relative.

An adult raccoon weighs from fifteen to twenty pounds and will live up to fourteen years in captivity. Seeing captive raccoons washing their food made us think for many years that all raccoons wash their food. We now realize that they do not; raccoons are seen fishing and playing with pebbles in the water, but a wild raccoon does not wash food before eating it.

Raccoons do not hibernate, but they do use their tree-house dens to sleep through severe winter weather. They are nocturnal animals who sleep through each day, rise at dusk, and then go back to sleep at dawn. When they wake up and greet the evening, they often utter a short wake-up cry that sounds a lot like a hoot owl. The raccoons are good hunters and foragers, and because of their adaptability and great strength, they will probably always be around.

Work Sheet 10-3

Venn Diagram

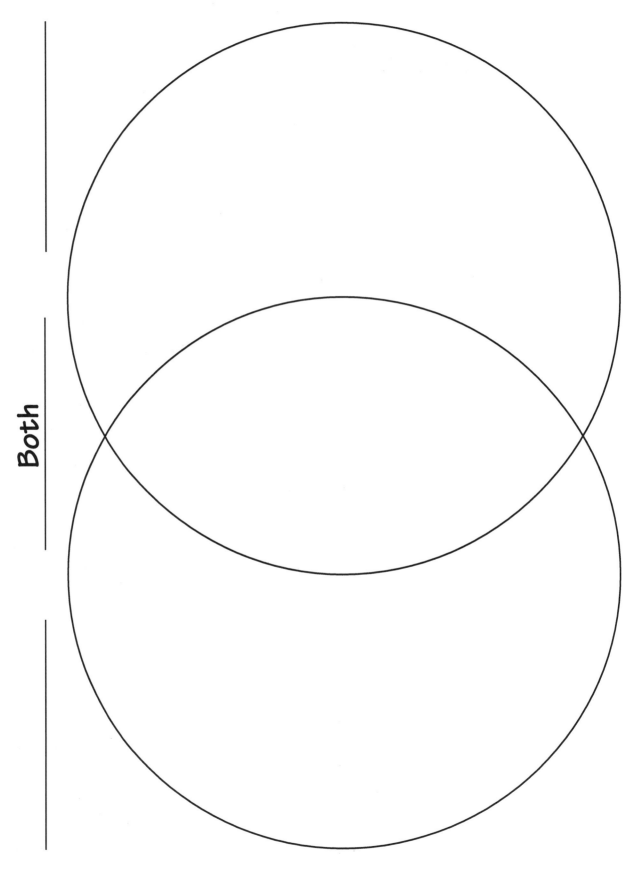

Section 3

Techniques

A teacher affects eternity; he can never tell where his influence stops.

—Henry Brooks Adams

FREE READING WITH LITERATURE CONNECTIONS

Grades K–6

If each student is reading his or her own literature selection on the subject of the unit's focus, classroom discussions will be far richer and more interesting than if all students were reading (or trying to read) the central literature selection. Following are a few suggestions for organizing this free reading time.

Primary Grades

Step 1: Use the literature connections list and your own school library to gather a wide variety of books that match the unit's focus.

Step 2: Each day let students spend 10 to 15 minutes reading or looking at a book from this collection. Be sure to include the books that you have read aloud to the class, as these will be the most prized. Students might read alone or in pairs or small groups to share and discuss what they are reading.

Step 3: Briefly review what all of their books have in common at the beginning of each free-reading period.

Step 4: At the end of each reading time, you might do one of the following:

Invite several students to tell the rest of the class what they liked about their books.

Ask students to read a favorite page or two aloud to their partners and then select a few students to read those pages aloud to the whole class.

Ask a few students to tell the class about their partner's books. (This sharing often increases students' interest in the books that their friends read aloud and talk about and might lead to your selection of the next day's read-aloud book.)

Step 5: If some students need reading assistance, they might listen to the text of one of the books (prerecorded by you or a student) at a listening post. Several students, not only your slower readers, could have this privilege each day.

More Challenge

Near the end of the unit of study, each student can select a favorite book from the collection and work with a partner or small group on a presentation for the class (see technique 8, Book Groups).

Intermediate Grades

Step 1: Let each student select a book from the literature connections list or your school library to read during a 20 to 30 minute silent reading period each day.

Step 2: At the end of every day's silent reading, ask one-fifth of your class to give one-minute oral reports on their books, to be followed immediately by questions from two or three other students. These questions serve both to keep the oral reports honest and to advertise all of the books to the rest of the class. You might wish to keep track of these oral reports on a class list for record-keeping and assessment purposes.

More Challenge

When students finish reading their individual books, assign a book report (see technique 12, Thoughtful Book Reports, on page 284).

Multiple Intelligence Connections

 READ-ALOUDS

Grades K–3

Preparation

For each day, select one picture book that is related to the unit's focus. Make a photocopy of the cover or title page, whichever has a more interesting picture.

Procedure

Step 1: Read one picture book aloud each day of the week. When you finish reading, show students the copy of the cover or the title page and ask for a volunteer to color it. Be sure this student puts his or her name on the back of the picture.

Step 2: When the picture has been colored, post it on a classroom wall.

Step 3: Add another book cover each day of the week. If you read more than one book aloud that is related to the unit's focus, add those book covers to the display also.

Step 4: On Monday, remind the class of all the read-alouds that are represented on your wall. Ask students to remember the stories in their imagination.

Step 5: Then ask each child to write (or draw a picture to represent) her or his favorite book title on a slip of paper or on individual chalkboards. Next, ask students to turn to study partners and tell why they like the books they chose.

Step 6: After students have committed to their choices, have them line up according to their selections to determine the classroom favorite book.

Step 7: Mount the picture of the book cover on a 9-by-12-inch sheet of colored art paper and add a ribbon and a gold seal. Mount the picture in a place of honor. The rest of the covers can be sent home with the children who colored them. If you continue this process, you will have a special bulletin board where the books of the week are displayed until the end of each quarter. In any newsletters that you send home, you can also let the parents know which books have been selected as favorites.

Optional Step 8: Instead of having students line up to indicate their choices, line the book covers up along the bottom of a bulletin board. Then ask each student to pin his or her voting paper above the book of choice. You will have a graph that indicates choices in mathematical language (see figure T-1).

Figure T-1. Students' votes for favorite read-alouds

Multiple Intelligence Connections

MUSIC CONNECTIONS

Music can add a great deal to the classroom atmosphere. In language arts classes it is especially fitting because songs are a form of literature. Providing opportunities for your students to sing has many linguistic benefits, including development of memorization skills, increased awareness of the meter and rhythm of words, and the provision of an enjoyable way for students of all ages to learn to read by reading something familiar again and again.

Preparation

Gather singable, enjoyable songs that correlate with the focus of your unit.

For grades 1 through 4, print each song on large chart paper, alternating the color of your marker every other line to help students follow along. You can hang each chart on the wall or attach it to a coat hanger to be stored and hung when necessary. You may also prepare a teacher-made big book with a line from the song on each page. Students may be recruited to illustrate these pages and the pages can be laminated.

For middle and upper grades, you may duplicate the words to each song for students to keep in personal music folders. Students may also practice handwriting by copying the words of each new song from the board.

Procedure

Step 1: During the course of the unit, introduce and teach these songs using the charts, big book format, or individual song sheets. For primary grades, at first you can point to each word as the class sings along with you, but soon students can be chosen for this task. For intermediate grades, encourage especially your low readers to point to each word on their song sheets as they sing, or to move a blank card to expose each new line as it is sung. This singing and tracking of words is a powerful strategy to improve reading ability.

Step 2: Periodically ask students to consider what these songs have in common. They may then wish to write unit-focused songs of their own. See unit 8, lesson 8: Writing a Camp Song, for suggestions on how to do this with your whole class.

Step 3: Once students have learned the song, add other musical accompaniment, such as bells, drums, kazoos, whistles, rhythm sticks, and so on. If you have access to a xylophone, keyboard, autoharp, or bells, students can work out a simple harmonic accompaniment by alternating the notes in the I, IV, and V7 chords that match each stanza.

Multiple Intelligence Connections

MAKING POCKET CHARTS

Grades K–6

Here is a way to create an inexpensive pocket chart that will last for several years.

Materials

a sheet of tagboard the size that you want your pocket chart to be

a roll of clear vinyl, available in the garden section of most variety stores

package-sealing tape

Procedure

Step 1: Cut the tagboard in the shape you desire.

Step 2: Cut the vinyl into strips 3 to 4 inches wide and 6 inches longer than the width of the tagboard.

Step 3: Tape the strips onto the tagboard beginning 6 inches below the top. Tape all the way along the bottom edge of the vinyl strip, allowing 3 inches to extend on either side of the tagboard (see figure T-2).

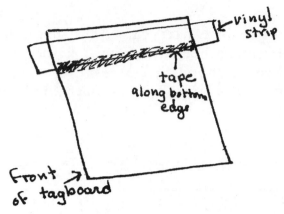

Figure T-2. Step 3 in making a pocket chart

Step 4: Turn the edges under and tape them in place on the back of the tagboard (see figure T-3).

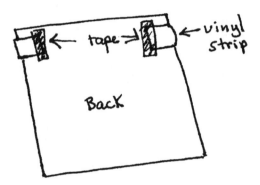

Figure T-3. Step 4 in making a pocket chart

Step 5: Continue to tape strips across the tagboard, working your way down in even increments to fit the size of the sentence strips you will be using (see figure T-4).

Figure T-4. The finished pocket chart

Multiple Intelligence Connections

Technique 5 — TEACHER-MADE BOOKS

Grades K–8

Many activities in these units call for teacher-made books. After primary students have completed their books, send the books home with the note to parents on page 275.

A Book with Room for Pictures

Step 1: Create books by alternating sheets of lined paper with sheets of art or blank paper.

Step 2: Cover the book with a colored construction paper cover and staple it along the left edge (see figure T-5). When the book is opened, students will have one page for writing and the opposite page for drawing.

 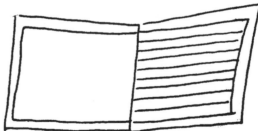

Figure T-5. A teacher-made picture book

A Writing-Only Book

Construct as for the picture book, but use lined paper only (see figure T-6). The number of pages will vary with the use for which each is intended.

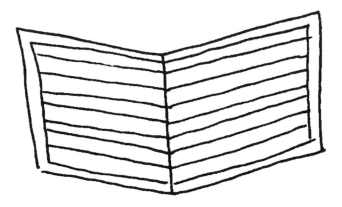

Figure T-6. A teacher-made writing-only book

Parent Note

Dear Parent,

As part of our study of children's literature, your child has written and illustrated this book. He or she should be able to read it to you, and I hope you will take the time to listen to it and discuss the words and the pictures. After your child reads this book to you, perhaps you can add it to your home library of children's books. In the future, you might sometimes choose to read this book along with those by more famous authors.

I hope you enjoy and express your pride in your child's work.

Sincerely,

SIGN LANGUAGE

The kinesthetic intelligence is another of those that Howard Gardner and many other educational leaders suggest that we try to incorporate in our teaching strategies. The addition of simple signing to a language arts program adds a kinesthetic element in a way that all students enjoy, with the benefit of also introducing a communication skill that may enable children to develop compassion and to communicate with those with hearing disabilities.

Learning the Signing Alphabet

The simplest path is to teach the signing alphabet. I teach it as I sing the alphabet song. Once students know the alphabet, they can use their fingers to respond to phonics questions or to indicate a choice from a list of words by signaling the first letter. When you are printing student-generated charts or doing group phonics work, you can ask all students to show you what the beginning consonant or the next letter of a word will be. Because all students are expected to show you, all students' brains engage. By quickly surveying the raised hands, you can easily tell who is not able to tell which letter is needed, and those students can then receive some one-on-one tutoring.

Singing with Signs for Words

Another natural ground for signing is to learn the signs for the words of songs or poems. You can get help in learning these signs from a parent or special education teacher who is familiar with signing, or from a book. I have found *Signing Exact English* by Gerilee Gustason, Donna Pfetzing, and Esther Zwaolkow, to be very helpful. Students of most ages enjoy signing the meaning of a song as they sing. It adds a delightful element to performances, as well.

Signing Directions

Signing can also be used to give simple classroom directions at all grade levels. It has a calming effect, as all eyes must focus on you before they take the next action.

Multiple Intelligence Connections

INTENTIONS AND
REFLECTIONS

Adding Metacognition to Projects

Whenever students are working on a project of their own choosing, whether for a single class period or for many days, the addition of this simple and speedy activity will add greatly to the effectiveness of the project and to a heightened sense of students' ownership and responsibility. This activity can be done each day of the project using a single sheet of paper or response journal page, or you can use the intentions and reflections work sheets mentioned in the units.

Step 1: At the start of each work period, students think and complete the following phrase: *Today I intend to . . .* They might finish the sentence with something like *design the shadow puppets and trace the designs onto the cardboard.* Walk around while students are writing to check that goals are realistic and that students have the materials they need to meet their goals. Star each paper you check as a signal for that student to begin working on the project.

Step 2: At the end of each work period, students reflect on their progress by completing the phrase *During this work period I . . .* They might finish the sentence with something like *did design most of the puppets, but I have one more to do tomorrow.*

Benefits

- Students have a better sense of their responsibility and do less floating around.

- Students have a better sense of the passage of the time allotted for the project as they regularly assess what they have done and what they still need to do.

- You are sure that all students have meaningful tasks and grasp what they need to do at the beginning of each work period.

- Self-evaluation is a valuable metacognitive activity that is added to whatever other thinking skills the project is enforcing, thus empowering students to take greater charge of their own learning.

Adaptation for Early Grades

Young students can draw pictures or use invented spelling to indicate their intentions. At the end of the work period, they can add a simple *yes, no,* or *some* to their papers to indicate their success. In addition to using this technique for projects, you can make it a valuable part of free play periods in grades 1 through 3. Each day, in a teacher-made journal using story paper, students indicate their choices of free-play activities by writing or drawing their intentions. At the end of the period, they draw or write a description of what they did. I ask students to date each page, and I send the journals home for students to share with parents at the end of each month. The result is more thoughtful student choices and a reading and writing link to a vital portion of the school day.

Multiple Intelligence Connections

 **BOOK GROUPS**

Grades 1–4

This technique is for use with primary-level picture books. The goal of this cooperative effort among students who have read and enjoyed the same book is to deepen comprehension and to increase the familiarity needed for beginning readers to strengthen their reading confidence and abilities.

Forming Groups

Have students self-select into the book groups by choosing a book that they have read and enjoyed. Your read-aloud selections are good options. If the group is large, it may elect to break into smaller groups.

Deciding on a Presentation Format

Once the groups are formed around the favored books, ask the class to help you make a list of things that can be done with books in order to present them to the class. Book groups work best approximately halfway through the school year, by which time your students will all be familiar with many different types of literature-related activities.

The list might include the following:

- Read the wall (see page 97, lesson 10 of *Over in the Meadow*).
- Do a theater presentation.
- Make costumes and scenery and memorize or read the story.
- Retell the story in a student-written and -illustrated book.
- Audiotape the story with sound effects.
- Make a model of the story and characters (clay, construction paper, and so on); group members take turns reading the story aloud, moving characters as needed.
- Make illustrations (overhead transparency, scroll, posters, and so on) and display them as the story is read aloud.
- Re-enact the story in your own words.

Working on the Presentation

This project will take a number of class periods. When the projects are ready, allow time for all groups to perform. Ask the audience for one or two compliments after each performance. You might wish to repeat the performances for parents or another teacher's class.

Multiple Intelligence Connections

VISUALIZATION

The transformation of dull letters and words on paper into a fully orchestrated mental image, complete with scenery, costumes, characters, and action, lies at the heart of the magic of reading. We don't learn how to read so that we can decode words and answer ten comprehension questions; we learn how to read so that we can see things that cannot be seen with our human eyes—ideas and activities from other times, other worlds, other perspectives.

Because most teachers are people who have always enjoyed reading and bringing words to life, it is hard to realize that one in five children does not know how to create the mental images that we take for granted. For many children, visualization strategies can make the vital difference between struggling with decoding and deciphering and truly reading with comprehension and pleasure.

Teaching young children to visualize is becoming more important. Many picture books have exceptional pictures, and we are so eager to show students these lovely illustrations. Students also encounter the pre-made pictures of television and movies, they lack time for inventive play, and they have too many toys that are linked with the specific plot of a movie or a cartoon. They aren't made to exercise their imaginations to create their own mental pictures of words. The lack of this skill makes the transfer to chapter books more difficult.

In the middle grades, many discouraged readers can get a fresh new start on reading through the use of visualization strategies. Once they see the print spring to life and take on personal meaning, they understand for the first time what reading is all about and their reading abilities often increase dramatically.

A quite natural time to foster visualization is during your oral reading if you insist upon students listening only (no drawing or distractions); students have nothing else to do but imagine. Another natural time is right before any creative writing. Instead of merely giving students a topic, such as "write a story about how the elephant got its trunk," allow a minute of silence for students to imagine the trunkless elephant walking through its jungle. Allow time for students to watch the event that would give this imaginary elephant his familiar trunk.

If a child has seldom or never visualized, it takes some work to begin the process. Following are some books that will help:

Rose, Laura. 1988. *Picture This (4–6): Teaching Reading through Visualization*. Tucson, Ariz.: Zephyr Press.
Teaches students from grades 4 through high school how to visualize to enhance their reading and creative writing. The book offers slow readers a fresh start, but is perfectly appropriate for middle and gifted students, as well.

———. 1991. *Picture This for Beginning Readers (K–3): Teaching Reading through Visualization*. Tucson, Ariz.: Zephyr Press.
Teaches beginning readers how to visualize as they learn to read and write.

———. 1992. *Folktales: Teaching Reading through Visualization and Drawing*. Tucson, Ariz.: Zephyr Press.

———. 1993. *Folktales Audiotapes: Teaching Reading through Visualization and Drawing*. Tucson, Ariz.: Zephyr Press.
Teaches students to visualize while they are reading by letting them vividly imagine and then illustrate each page of a traditional folktale. Effective with grades K through 5.

Multiple Intelligence Connections

RESPONSE JOURNALS

The response journals for these units can be teacher-made books (see technique 5, Teacher-Made Books, page 273) or any notebook or composition book. Three vital elements contribute to an effective response journal:

1. Students write their thoughtful responses to the literature.

2. The teacher writes a response to the students' comments in a conversational way to motivate students to respond further in a genuine communication of thoughts and feelings.

3. The teacher evaluates in order to motivate and bases the evaluation on full participation rather than merely on correct spelling, correct grammar, or correct answers.

When the unit is over, you might ask students to evaluate and grade their own response journals. This self-evaluation helps students develop a sense of responsibility for their own work. If you post a list on the board or overhead of how many entries of what length have been required, students can go through their journals, add up their points, and give themselves a grade. Some teachers include an evaluation sheet at the start of each response journal to inform students how they will be held accountable (see example below).

Chapter 1	at least one-half page response	10 points
Chapter 4	detailed picture of boat	
	one-half page description of its success or failure	20 points
Chapter 5	drawing of plants, stone, scarf	10 points
	math to find size of island	15 points

The evaluation criteria are usually based on full participation, rather than on correct answers. If students evaluate their own journals, you can verify their self-assigned grades when you collect the books.

Note: For more information about response journals, refer to Response Journals, Les Parsons, Heinemann Press.

Multiple Intelligence Connections

  WRITING OPINION PAPERS

Grades 4–6

Use the following format to provide a simple way to help students form and express opinions clearly and convincingly.

To Teach the Format to Students

Step 1: Make an overhead transparency of work sheet 7-3 or duplicate the five steps on a chalkboard or large chart paper, leaving room for writing your paragraphs.

Step 2: Pick a topic and write the paper as students watch and help, conforming to each of the steps as you write (see example below).

First Paragraph: State your opinion and three reasons to justify it.

I would like to remain a child forever instead of growing up. I don't really want to have to go to work every day. I don't want to stop being silly and having fun, and I would rather be the kid than the mom.

Second Paragraph: Expand on your first reason.

I don't want to grow up and have to go to work every day. I like school because my friends are here and I get to go home at 3:00 and I get summers off. But my mom and dad have to work eight hours every day and they have to work in the summer and Christmas vacation.

Third paragraph: Expand on your second reason.

I've noticed that grown-ups don't get silly and have fun like kids do. They don't have slumber parties and stay up half the night eating popcorn and watching videos. They don't roller skate and when they exercise, they are so serious. I'd rather stay silly and have fun.

Fourth paragraph: Expand on your third reason.

I wouldn't want to have all the work of being a mom and dad. Sometimes my brother can really be a nuisance, and they have to yell at him and clean up after him. I do some chores, but my mom and dad have to do a lot more, and I don't want to work that hard, even though I would like to have a baby some day.

Fifth paragraph: Restate your opinion and close.

So I have to say although there are some good things about growing up, like earning money and having a baby of your own, I would rather stay a kid forever if I had to make a choice.

Step 3: Let students use the same format to write a paper expressing their own opinions. You might wish to let them use copies of work sheet 7-3 for their first try or if you are working with younger children.

Use this technique to engage students with any literature selection of your choice.

Multiple Intelligence Connections

Technique 12

THOUGHTFUL BOOK REPORTS

Grades 3–8

When assigning book reports, we sometimes get into a rut and expect an identical form after every book is read. On the other hand, broader menus of the book report option tend to be almost entirely of the creative family: make a poster, make a diorama, write a play, paint a poster, or write a new ending.

We might stimulate more thought and understanding if we asked our students to report on their books using activities selected from the four thinking domains:

Mastery

- Write a summary.

- Write an outline.

- Memorize and recite a segment.

- Audiotape a segment with sound effects to play to the class.

- Practice oral reading and perform a favorite segment.

- Make a list of new words encountered in this book and their definitions.

- Locate the story on a map and show where each story element took place.

- Create an overhead-view map of the story.

- Find some examples of a particular literary device in your story, such as alliteration, metaphor, simile, personification, exaggeration, or other devices.

Reasoning

- Use a Venn diagram to compare two characters from the book.

- Use a Venn diagram to compare this book with the central literature selection.

- Analyze why the author wrote the book.

- Write one sentence for each of the main story elements or chapters.

- Tell how you think the author was biased and give evidence.

- Write an opinion paper to agree or disagree with a story element or the author's position.

Personal Connection

- Keep a journal and write personal responses to each chapter or event.

- Make a double entry-journal of one event from each chapter paired with a similar event from your own life or with a few sentences telling how the incident made you feel.

- Act out all or part of the story for the class or on videotape.

- Choose your favorite chapter and tell why you like it best.

- List the five best, most exciting, or boring features of this book.

- Give a short talk to convince someone else to read the book (tell what you like about the book to convince someone else to read it). Do not tell the ending.

- Interview friends or family about events similar to those in the book.

Creation

- If you do not like the ending, write an ending you would prefer.

- Draw illustrations for the main story elements and make a story board.

- Create an artistic representation of the book: a mobile, a mural, a diorama, a poster, a painting, a comic-book version, or another creative rendition.

- Draw portraits of the main characters.

- Write a ballad that tells the story.

Given this wide array of book report options, you might choose to give students the following options:

- A choice of any of the above formats.

- For each book reporting assignment, a choice between the activities in only one thinking domain, rotating that domain with each new reporting period.

- Once a quarter, a choice of book-reporting format from each of the thinking domains; do them all with one book selection.

- A choice of reporting mechanisms, but insist on a different thinking domain with each new book.

Multiple Intelligence Connections

Technique 13

WEBBING FOR RESEARCH REPORTS

Grades 3–6

Step 1: Create an overhead transparency from work sheet 9 or draw a similar framework on chart paper or chalkboard and duplicate work sheet 10-1 for each student.

Step 2: Record your research topic, such as "Finding Out about Rabbits," in the center circle.

Step 3: Ask students what they might like to know about the topic, and record their questions in the circles that radiate out from the topic (see example on page 287).

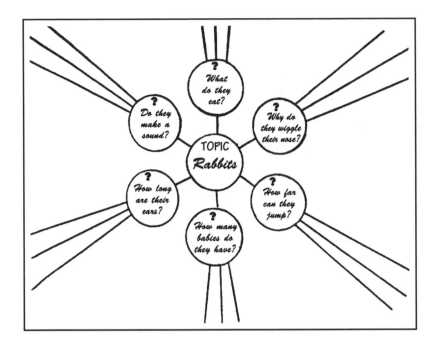

Step 4: Students can then copy your questions onto their work sheets, create different questions of their own, or some combination of the two. They may all be researching the same topic as your model, or they may each have their own central focus with similar questions.

Step 5: As students do the research with the whole class, in groups, or individually, they can answer each of their recorded questions in the lines that extend from each circle. If some students want to research more questions, they can use a second copy of the form or draw a web of their own. If they need more room to write, they can tape more paper along the sides of the forms.

Step 6: When all questions have been researched and the answers recorded, each author can use his or her webbing work sheet as a reference for creating any number of presentations, such as written reports, oral reports, newscasts, comic books, student-written nonfiction books, poems, mobiles, and countless others.

Section

4

Conclusion

In everything we ought to look to the end.

—Jean de La Fontaine

The *Developing Intelligences through Literature* units are designed to teach children how to think more deeply about what they read and write. I strongly believe that children learn how to read by reading and reading and reading. If we put high-quality books into our students' hands and provide extended time for them to read, read, read, their reading skills will almost certainly grow. But students need instruction in how to process the information they glean from their reading, and students of all learning styles need to be thoughtfully engaged in meaningful activities.

Children need to be taught to be critical in their assessment of written and oral messages. They need to be encouraged to apply the meanings of stories to their own lives so that they can learn from the experience and wisdom of others. They need to be guided to examine their readings from an author's perspective so that they can assimilate and utilize the wide array of writing skills for their creative self-expression. They need to be encouraged to bring words and concepts to life in their unique imaginations. If you organize your literature-based units around these kinds of thinking skills you will help your students to be not only skilled and enthusiastic readers, but critical, creative, productive members of our world.

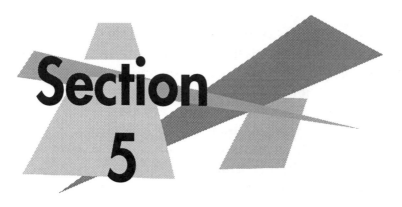

Section 5

Create Your Own Units Using This Model

It is wise to learn; it is God-like to create.

—John Saxe

Select a Central Work of Literature and a Focus

Many books are fun to read, but you will select only a few each year to delve into with the intensity that a unit of study provides. These units engage all students in rich interactions with the text and provide a fertile ground in which they can exercise and deepen their various intelligences. Therefore from time to time we want to select a book that leads us into a meaningful focus.

Sometimes the concept will come first and you will seek literature to help you address it. Other times a piece of literature will catch your interest and then you will decide the focus of the unit. Following are examples of connections with rich potential:

> *A social studies focus:* Little House on the Prairie *for pioneer spirit*
>
> *A math-related focus:* Over in the Meadow *for learning to read numbers in primary grades*
>
> *A science-related focus:* Huckleberry Finn *for learning to read dialect*
>
> *A literature-pattern focus:* If You Give a Mouse a Cookie *for a circular story*
>
> *A biographical focus:* Helen Keller
>
> *A citizenship focus:* Johnny Tremain *for honesty and hard work*
>
> *A human potential focus:* Call It Courage *or* Keep the Lights Burning, Abbie *for courage*

The selection of such a clear focus has several benefits:

- It helps you to choose from among the limitless array of literature activities.

- It helps students see meaning in the unit of study. It helps the unit progress toward a definite closure; students can say, "This is what I learned from this unit."

- It helps you connect your in-depth literature study to concepts that you need to teach your students.

Exceptions to the Rule: Kindergarten and First Grades

For beginning readers, a meaningful focus is not as important as the selection of a unit that has a strong appeal to children. The purpose of a primary-grade study unit is to engage children in exciting, age-appropriate activities that further their positive involvement with reading and writing. Although dinosaurs have very little impact on children's lives today, nonetheless a unit on dinosaurs is the very thing to excite and involve every child.

Brainstorm a Related-Literature List

Create a list of other fiction and nonfiction books, articles, short stories, music, or poems with your focus. Your librarian can help you. I have also included a list of reference books (page 296) that can help you find literature that is related to many specific topics. You might also list kits or other materials that relate to your unit focus: art prints, science kits, film, videos, posters, and such.

Before beginning your unit, collect the literature so that your students can make independent reading choices. Some of it may give you further ideas for unit activities.

Decide How to Present the Literature to Your Students

Decide whether you will read the book aloud to your students or if they will read it themselves. All units in this books are based on the teacher reading the central literature selection aloud so that all students, regardless of reading ability, have equal access to the author's idea.

Teach and Enjoy

Do as many of the lessons you have brainstormed, striving for balance between the thinking domains of mastery, personal connection, reasoning, creation, and metacognition. Notice when enthusiasm about the topic begins to fade. A unit of study can be as brief as a single day and still have impact.

Appendixes

Appendix A

A Brief Synopsis of Howard Gardner's Seven Intelligences

Howard Gardner names seven intelligences and proposes that these intelligences be deliberately included in curriculum for the inclusion of all kinds of learners and the expansion of their thinking and learning potential. These seven are not an exclusive list, but their use in classrooms will greatly enhance student involvement and thinking development. Many excellent teaching lessons will include several of these intelligences.

 Musical/Rhythmic: Students sing, dance, listen, and respond to music. They develop musical abilities and talents and learn to distinguish tone, mood, melody, and rhythm. Rhyme, rap, chanting, dance, songs, and jump-rope rhymes are all ways to access this intelligence.

 Bodily/Kinesthetic: Students learn through touch and movement. Field trips, math and science manipulatives, gymnastics, role-playing, sign language, and many artistic and physical expressions provide access to this intelligence.

 Interpersonal: Students learn through developing empathy and connection with other humans. Cooperative learning, interviews, partner-reading, inferences based on oral and body language, discussions, and group problem solving are ways to access this intelligence.

 Intrapersonal: Students learn through increased awareness of their own interests, abilities, and strengths. Metacognition, development of increased self-esteem and self-awareness, pride, and self-evaluation of work all are part of this intelligence.

 Visual/Spatial: Students learn through perceiving three-dimensional reality. Visualization, architectural planning, orienting by maps and directional cues, planning and executing mazes, imaging story maps, and planning three-dimensional projects all access this intelligence.

 Logical/Mathematical: Students learn through reasoning and logic. Sequencing, scientific thinking, cause and effect awareness, mathematical reasoning, and number sense are all parts of this intelligence.

 Verbal/Linguistic: Students learn through the use of language communication skills. Reading, writing, oral speech, persuasion, phonics, spelling, and other composition skills are all part of this intelligence.

If you are interested in delving further into these ideas, following are some books you might explore:

Armstrong, Thomas. 1994. *Multiple Intelligences in the Classroom*. ASCD.

Campbell, Bruce, Linda Campbell, and Dee Dickinson. 1992. *Teaching and Learning through Multiple Intelligences*. Campbell.

New City School. 1994. *Multiple Intelligences: Teaching for Success*.

Appendix B

Reference Books for Locating Children's Books by Topic

Baskins, Barbar. *Notes from a Different Drummer*. Bowker.
Includes longer books and some picture books. Focuses on children with special needs. Extensive reviews.

Bauer, Carolyn Feller. *Celebrations*. Wilson.
Includes picture books and longer books.

———. *Handbooks for Storytellers*. Wilson.
Concerned only with picture books.

———. *This Way to Books*. Wilson.
Includes picture books and longer books.

Bernstein, Joanne E. *Books to Help Children Cope with Separation and Loss*. Bowker.
Includes longer books, some picture books. Treats books that cover a wide range of losses, from minor to major. Brief reviews.

California State Department of Education. *Recommended Readings in Literature*.
Includes picture books and longer books listed by broad topics. Brief synopses.

Carroll, Frances. *Exciting, Funny, Scary, Short, Different, and Sad Books Kids Like . . .* ALA.
Includes longer books for readers through grade 6. Plot synopses.

———. *Guide to Subject and Concepts in Picture Book Format*. Oceanna.
Picture books listed by subject matter or concept rather than by social or emotional.

Colborn, Candace. 1994. *What Do Children Read Next?* Gale.

Dreyer, Sharon Spredemann. 1982. *The Best of Bookfinder*. American Guidance.

Lima, Carolyn, and John Lima. *A to Zoo*. Bowker.
Includes picture books listed by encyclopedic topics rather than by social or emotional topics.

Lipson, Eden. New York Times *Parent's Guide to the Best Books for Children*. Times.
Includes picture books and longer books. Plot synopses. Subject index.

Lynn, Ruth N. *Fantasy Literature for Children and Young Adults*. Bowker.
Longer books for readers through grade 12. Plot synopses.

NCTE. *Adventuring with Books.*
> Includes picture books and longer books. Arranged by subject. Brief reviews.

Spredemann, Sharon. *Bookfinder.* AGS.
> Includes longer books, some picture books listed by subject. Lengthy reviews and comments.

———. *Subject Guide to Children's Books in Print.* Bowker.
> Includes picture books, longer books for readers through young adults. Lists all books in print on each topic without restriction or evaluation.

Tway, Eileen. *Reading Ladders for Human Relations.* NCTE.
> Includes picture books and longer books for readers through young adults. Lists only books that treat social issues.

Notes